4.50

THE MUTATION OF EUROPEAN CONSCIOUSNESS AND SPIRITUALITY

THE MUTATION OF EUROPEAN CONSCIOUSNESS AND SPIRITUALITY

From the Mythical to the Modern

Willy Obrist

KARNAC

First published in German in 2006 by Opus Magnum, Stuttgart

First published in English in 2014 by
Karnac Books Ltd
118 Finchley Road, London NW3 5HT

British Library Cataloguing in Publication Data

A C.I.P. for this book is available from the British Library

  ISBN 978 1 78220 080 2

Translation by Reinhard Buerger

Edited, designed and produced by The Studio Publishing Services Ltd
www.publishingservicesuk.co.uk
e-mail: studio@publishingservicesuk.co.uk

Printed in Great Britain

www.karnacbooks.com

CONTENTS

Willy Obrist (1918–2013) studied philosophy, history, and medicine, and became an enthusiastic scientist in the field of human studies. After he had worked for a number of years as an internist (specialising in angiology) in his own practice in Switzerland, he decided to study depth psychology and completed his studies by becoming a training analyst. From 1970 to 1990, he was a lecturer at the C. G. Jung Institute in Zurich. He was a member of staff of the Stiftung für Humanwissenschaftliche Grundlagenforschung (Zurich), conducting fundamental research focusing on the evolution of consciousness. Willy Obrist was a co-founder of the Swiss Society of Religious Studies, of the Foundation of Analytical Psychology (Zurich), and of the Foundation to Foster Philosophy (Mönchengladbach, Germany).

Since the 1970s, I have been fascinated by exploring the fundamental change of the European conception of the world and of man that has taken place since the beginning of the Modern Age (about 1500). As this process that I want to deal with is extremely complex, I decided to describe its various aspects in several steps—which meant five books—to grasp the meaning of this process as comprehensively as possible.

In each book, the essence of the whole work is outlined, but each time a different aspect of this epoch-making change is given priority. *The Mutation of Consciousness* (1980) mainly depicts the initial situation—the supernaturalistic, archaic worldview—by means of examples taken from ethnography and the history of religion.

The question "How can I go on living religiously in spite of the new, modern, naturalistic worldview?" demands an extensive description of the various schools of spirituality in the different world religions.

By doing so, I could show that man's ability to develop a religious attitude belongs to the repertoire of behaviour of the species homo sapiens. This pattern of behaviour is independent of the worldview valid at that time. The nature of religiousness is the topic of the second book: *New Consciousness and Religiousness* (1988).

The discovery of the unconscious played a decisive role in the context of the mutation of occidental consciousness but the theoretical systematisation of depth psychology had not satisfyingly been realised yet in the 1970s. So, this problem had to be dealt with in a separate book: *Archetypes* (1990). There is a great number of theologians' prejudices against the way depth psychology conceives human psyche. My efforts to overcome these misunderstandings resulted in the book *Depth Psychology and Theology* (1993). Finally, the core of the mutation of consciousness—the change of the conception of the two pairs of terms: "matter–mind", "body–mind"—asked for an even more comprehensive analysis. The title I had suggested for the book about that topic was: "No matter without mind". For commercial reasons, however, the publisher changed the title to: *Nature – A Source of Ethics and Meaning* (1999).

After these publications, my work about the change of the European worldview seemed to be complete, according to my opinion. Besides, my work had become quite extensive. However, as today's flood of information seems to hinder many people from investing enough time to read a book thoroughly and to get a grip on the conceptions presented, I was repeatedly asked to write a brief, concise, clear summary of my essential ideas and insights, and I agreed.

Introduction

The change in the European worldview was radical. A fundamental pattern of understanding oneself and the world that had been the basis of all cultures since the Stone Age has been overcome and replaced by a fundamentally new conception. Nevertheless, we must be aware that the old worldview is still the basis of most non-European cultures nowadays. This process began at the end of our Middle Ages and needed 500 years to develop. The fundamental change that occurred under the surface of phenomena to which historians have access can only be realised and understood when considered from the point of view of consciousness evolution.

This new point of view enables us to realise developments different from those analysed by the traditional method relating to intellectual history. From the new point of view, we can become conscious of deep, complex, far-reaching processes. At the same time, it becomes obvious that this collective process follows the same laws of psychic change that an individual's change follows.

The evolution of consciousness is, indeed, a natural phenomenon, just like individuation. Individuation, in biological terms, means to realise one's species-specific programme in one's individual life. When becoming aware of the evolution of consciousness, we can also see it as the last phase of the world's entire evolution: a tremendous process of constantly increasing complexity of space–time systems which has advanced inexorably: at first as the evolution of matter, then the evolution of unconscious living beings, and, finally, as the evolution of consciousness after man had appeared.

Considering the change of the occidental worldview as an evolutionary step, we can regard it as a step to a more subtly differentiated conception of nature and man. This step can be called a mutation, even a mega mutation in analogy with other corresponding events in the evolution of living beings. One has to be aware, however, that mutations in the context of the evolution of consciousness take place on the basis of tradition and not of genomes.

Although the mutation of occidental consciousness had already begun in the Renaissance, its breakthrough was not realised before the twentieth century. Even today, the new conception of the world and man that has emerged is hardly known. Evolutionary breakthroughs just occur at the top of the consciousness of a population and then slowly spread in the course of generations.

It is the intention of this little book to enhance the diffusion of this new worldview.

In order to attain this aim, first I outline the methodical approach to exploring the evolution of consciousness, because the consideration from this new point of view is the key to understanding the deep-reaching process that is the topic of this book.

Second, I describe the archaic worldview: the fundamental pattern of the conception of oneself and the world which all former cultures were based on, and which is, for example, still the basis of Islamic and Hindu cultures today.

Third, how the evolution of consciousness developed during the archaic phase is shown. I especially refer to the fact that in the philosophy of Christian scholasticism that had constantly refined the conception of objective mind, this conception was imprisoned in its self-made boundaries because of its concrete way of thinking. So, evolution could only advance if a fundamentally new and no longer concrete conception of the two essential pairs of terms, matter–mind and body–mind, was found.

After these three chapters, the long search in the Modern Age for a new way to conceive our world is depicted. Looking at this process, we will realise that the mutation of consciousness has followed the same laws of psychic change that can be observed when we accompany an individual's psychic development. In depth psychology, the laws of this process are called the laws of antithetical tension and transcending function.

The mutation of consciousness took place in two steps: The first step was caused by the progress of empirical–scientific research and the reflections of the philosophers of the Enlightenment that led to the antithetical tension between the opposing positions of the archaic and positivistic worldview: the so-called dilemma between knowledge and faith.

The second step transcended this dilemma in the course of the twentieth century and resulted in a new concept of man and his world. By means of this breakthrough, the archaic as well as the positivistic–materialistic worldview were questioned and relativised.

It can also be stated that in our century some still valuable elements of these old positions could be integrated into a basically new, evolutionarily higher conception of the world, due to discoveries and evolutionary acquisitions made in the meantime (Figure 1).

Although the empirical proof of the reality of the human unconscious that was produced by Sigmund Freud and Carl Gustav Jung at the beginning of the twentieth century led to the breakthrough of a new understanding of man, the theoretical foundations and specific terms of *Tiefenpsychologie*—depth psychology—were and still are relatively scarcely spread or made known. (In many countries, Jung's analytical psychology is not taught at universities: for example, neither in Germany nor in Switzerland.) That is why I explain its most important terms in a separate chapter.

As I think it is very helpful to understanding the new worldview better when we first focus on the evolutionary change of the concept of matter and mind, especially the aspect of objective mind, I concentrate on this aspect: objective mind is the mind that had been there before consciousness, or, in other words, before the subjective mind came into being. Furthermore, in the context of the new conception of our self and our world, the fundamentally new understanding of the source of ethical norms and the new spirituality resulting from it is discussed: this spirituality that corresponds with today's level of consciousness is "religiousness without religion".

Finally, I shall make you aware of the enormous consequences of the breakthrough to this fundamentally new worldview, and I also point out that we have to take into account that there is still a long way to go until most people realise that we are not just living at the threshold of a new age, but of a radically new age.

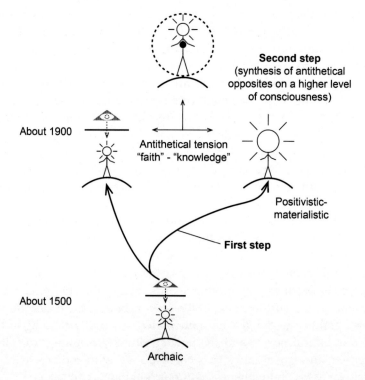

Figure 1. The two steps in the mutation of consciousness.

CHAPTER ONE

Initial situation

T he term "theory of evolution" is used for two different processes: one, to describe the empirically proved fact that a constant increase of the complexity of spatio–temporal systems has taken place, and two, to describe the models which try to explain the reasons for this evolution.

At the beginning, I shall deal with the first meaning of evolution, which means a description of how this process has developed. The question of what might have caused the evolution will be answered at the end in the context of the discussion of the new conception of the pair of terms, matter–mind. Then it will become obvious that the materialistic theory of evolution as promoted by Darwin and his pupils has been supplanted by the second step of the mutation. This new view is by no means a regression into the archaic creationism of the kind that is still taught in some parts of the USA today.

A discussion of the evolution of human mind had taken place many years before Darwin proved the evolution of animal beings. The process concerning the human mind was still called cultural evolution, though. Hence, it was quite understandable that mainly scholars of human sciences or of philosophy presented models about cultural development and evolution. These theories were rejected vehemently by people who were intensely annoyed at the idea of cultural evolution. Theologians, especially, attacked this view of human history because they seemed to realise subconsciously that, from this new point of view, the branch they were sitting on would be sawn off.

The concepts of the scholars in the humanities could easily be refuted verbally because their methodical approach was insufficiently founded, which means that their approach did not provide a measure to define the degree of the evolutionary level that had been reached. In the 1970s, I finally succeeded, in co-operation with the Stiftung für Humanwissenschaftliche Grundlagenforschung (SHG), in conceiving a methodical approach that has a good grasp of the phenomenon of culture. This approach is no longer speculatively or philosophically founded, but is scientifically based. In its new terminology, the term "cultural evolution" is replaced by "evolution of consciousness". The cognitive system that has developed enables man to produce culture that is independent of its object. Culture independent of its object means: cultural achievements cannot be realised and passed on merely by showing somebody something and the other one imitating it, as is still the case with the few "discoveries" achieved by today's chimpanzee.

The new methodical approach is based on the following train of thought: in order to define the degree of complexity or the evolutionary level of a system, one has to know its basic qualities; the system in question may be molecular, alive, or cognitive. Unfortunately, the qualities of the cognitive system "consciousness" cannot be defined by observing and analysing today's man because his consciousness, as it is today, is the result of a long evolutionary process in whose course secondary capacities such as syntax, abstract, final, and logical thinking have been acquired. So, the evolutionary origins of consciousness had to be looked for somewhere else.

It was known from the systemic observation of evolution that at each step from a simpler to a more complex system, new qualities emerged, qualities that had never been seen before.

Konrad Lorenz, the famous Austrian behavioural scientist (1903–1989), created the term "fulguration" to describe the emergence of something new, a term derived from the Latin word *fulgur*—lightning. To define the basic qualities, one had to find out which new capacities had been added to the already highly complex cognitive capacities of the evolutionarily highest developed vertebrate at the step from unconscious to conscious living beings, which means at the step from animal to man.

Besides that, it was known that each time such a step was necessary in a phylogenetic group, a kind of groping for something new began. Consequently, it had to be asked if something like groping for consciousness could be detected before consciousness appeared on earth in our phylogenetic group. Chimpanzees, our phylogenetically closest relatives, were the candidates for our experiments to find out about that. Indeed, the mirror experiments showed that chimpanzees have cognitive capacities which other euglena do not have yet. Lower euglena often attack their reflections in the mirror, because they think they are to be their rivals, whereas the chimpanzees recognise themselves in the mirror. The cognitive capacity that becomes obvious in this fulguration is known as the capacity to distinguish between the ego and the non-ego, between subject and object. That means this capacity is the characteristic quality of consciousness.

However, the evolution of the chimpanzee stopped at this most primitive level of consciousness. The breakthrough to complete consciousness took place only on the branch of development that led to homo sapiens, and only within this species—our species—has the further progress of the evolution of consciousness up to today's level taken place.

As we are forced by the structure of our consciousness to make distinctions and conceive pairs of terms, if we want to understand objective reality, we have to consider two aspects when looking at man's capacity to distinguish between the ego and the non-ego: first, to recognise ourselves as something separate from the non-ego, in other words, from objective reality, and second, to realise and make distinctions within the non-ego which man perceives. These capacities advance man's consciousness and help him to penetrate the mere façade of outer appearance. For both capacities of human consciousness, true evolutionary progress could scientifically be proved.

Something else had to be taken into account. Since the beginning of evolution, since the "big bang", the increase of complexity has always run parallel to diversification. While a diversification of species took place in the evolution of biological organisms, so did a diversification of cultures in the evolution of consciousness. While a species is defined as a group whose members do not mate with the individuals of a group of a different species, this is not true for human cultures, in which mingling is almost a characteristic or typical trait. Often, even, a creative step forward is caused by an amalgamation of different cultures.

Besides, we must remember that achievements of biological evolution are passed on to further generations by means of genomes, while new capacities or discoveries achieved in the course of the evolution of consciousness are passed on through tradition. Due to man's capacity to express himself verbally, he can communicate and share his new insights with others. The achievements can be preserved safely in the memory of the group members just as, for example, they might be stored by means of books or electronic technology. Future generations will be able to adopt and extend the wide range of information during their socialisation, and when they discover something unknown, they can add their new insights to the old store of information and capacities.

In addition, there is still the difference of constancy of biological species and of human cultures. Species can stay the same for millions of years. With cultures, however, there is always *aggiornamento* (Italian: adaptation, modernisation). In this process, outdated points of view are dropped. For this reason, the evolution of consciousness cannot be reconstructed as completely as the biological evolution of living beings. To a certain degree, this lack can be compensated for by the fact that geographically separated cultures have developed at different speeds. Owing to this fact, it has become possible in recent years to observe and analyse early phases of human development, and even today various ethnic groups have remained at outdated levels of cultural development in spite of modern communication technology. This is caused by a neophobic tendency which is opposed to *aggiornamento*, or, in other words, is an unconscious resistance against a greater awareness of oneself and of one's world.

Let us now turn to the question of how the exploration of the evolution of consciousness proceeded. Scientists accepted as a starting point that man is able to create culture due to his consciousness. The degree of the capacity to distinguish between the ego and the non-ego that became visible in his culture informed scientists about the degree of complexity of the cognitive system, which relates to the complexity of the consciousness of the people who had created the culture in question.

Scientists could use the results of cultural studies, but they had to look at cultures from a point of view different from the one that is traditionally taken by cultural historians. While historians aim to present all the different aspects of cultures and the specific differences between them, the scientists who want to explore the evolution of consciousness just ask one question: what is the degree of the capacity to distinguish between the ego and the non-ego as expressed in the culture in question?

The archaic conception of ourselves and of our world

Beforehand, one other problem had to be solved in this approach to culture. This problem arose from the fact that in early and foreign cultures, people's concepts and methods of thinking were radically different from today's concepts. For this reason, not only the statements, concepts, and ideas of the so-called primitive people can hardly be understood by us nowadays, but also those of the theologians of the main world religions.

This difficulty is caused by the fact that the very early concepts and ways of thinking were based on conditions very different from ours today. People were led—and some are still led—by different "preconnections".

Before defining the degree of the capacity of distinction as it was expressed in people's conception of themselves and their world, their basic structure of thinking had to be explored. Because of the extraordinary variety of cultures and religious conceptions, it seemed as if this aim could not be achieved.

That was the point when I asked myself if there was not a common basic pattern underlying the diverse concepts of oneself and of one's world that had developed in geographically different areas through many different phases of human history, and, indeed, through intercultural comparisons such a paradigm could be shown. In order to distinguish it from today's new worldview, I called it the archaic (Greek *archaios*: old, outdated) conception of ourselves and of our world.

However, it was not sufficient merely to recognise this paradigm. In order to define the degree of the capacity to distinguish between the ego and the non-ego that had been reached in a culture, the inner logical structure of that way of thinking had to be explored and understood. The key to the solution of this problem was "depth psychology", the new type of empirical science that had emerged with the discovery of the unconscious. Due to its decryption of the language of the unconscious, it has become possible to translate archaic trains of thoughts into current concepts of thinking, and that has enabled us to understand the symbolic language that is used as a code in dreams, visions, daydreams, and in the myths which have resulted from them. It was interesting to realise that many archaic conceptions, mainly the so-called religious myths, are true: not physically true, as people thought from their archaic point of view, but psychically true. That means they contain true insights about psychic phenomena and laws encoded in a symbolic or metaphorical language.

Now a brief outline of the basic pattern of people's archaic conception of themselves and of their world will follow. For a more extensive explanation illustrated with examples, the reader is invited to turn to my book *The Mutation of Consciousness*.

Later, when the theoretical basis of depth psychology is presented, the development of the archaic pre-connections will be dealt with, and it will become obvious that the radical about-face of these pre-connections is the core of the process which I call the mutation of consciousness.

A characteristic trait of the archaic worldview (Figure 2) is the distinction between two worlds, or two spheres of reality: the visible world and the invisible one. People have also used other pairs of terms to describe these two spheres: worldly–unworldly, natural–supernatural, physical–metaphysical, immanent–transcendent.

It was believed that the other world was inhabited by invisible beings. On the one hand, there were the autochthonous beings that had always been gods and intermediate beings such as angels and demons, and, on the other hand, there were the dead who had once lived in this world and then passed on to live in the world hereafter.

Archaic people ascribed three capacities to the other-worldly beings: first, the capacity to have an impact on our world here and now acausally by mere thinking and will. Second, the ability to communicate with human beings and to reveal themselves to them. Third, to incarnate, which means to adopt a carnal, physical body. They were believed to be able to reveal themselves in three ways: first, by means of a striking omen in nature or in oracles. Second, in the fate that happened to an individual person or to a community, to a whole people. Third, in the main form of revelation: visions and dreams.

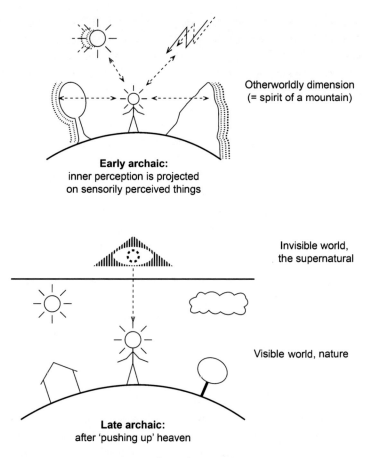

Figure 2. The archaic worldview.

While these revelations happened supernaturally from the archaic point of view, it seemed that during its incarnation a godly being was able to communicate with a human being in a completely natural way. In theological theory, however, at least in Christian theology, these messages were also considered to be supernatural because they had been uttered by godly beings.

All knowledge about the other world, and even some knowledge about this world here and now, was attributed to the process of revelation, and theologies emerged from reflection about revelation. Since the discovery of the unconscious—in other words, since man's awareness of human inner perception—all the information, stories, or events that seemed to be "revealed" to people by a supernatural world have been called myths: that is, creations of the unconscious that have manifested themselves historically. Within these myths, we distinguish between religious myths, which deal with other-worldly beings and their activities, and explanatory myths, which "interpret" the processes of nature or the origin and history of a tribe or a people.

As archaic people supposed the other-worldly beings to be superior to them and to control their actions, they tried hard to adopt a religious (Latin *religere*: to feel obliged, to respect, to esteem) attitude towards these superior beings: that is, to respect their will whenever a decision had to be made. From the collective endeavour to realise this attitude, religions originated. We can describe them as socio-cultural formations that are based on the archaic worldview. They are spiritual communities with fixed ideas about the world hereafter and set patterns of behaviour connected with these ideas. These ideas form the contents of their faith and the patterns consist of magical practices and rites. The members of these communities have a certain self-conception based on their experience of participation (e.g., the Catholic church as the mystic body of Christ). Magic and the rites were based on the idea that certain people could execute acausal power, too.

Man affected changes to things by means of his own power through magic practices by telling and showing things how they should be. These practices belonged to a low level of the evolution of consciousness. They were an expression of the hardly developed capacity of the ego to recognise itself as something different from the non-ego. On this level, man experienced his unconscious mainly outside, in projection, and he felt threatened by an immense number of invisible powers. He countered these threats with magic sayings and gestures to repel them, or to make them amenable. In addition to that, man still felt more closely related to his group, and less separated from plants and animals and from earth, waters, and mountains. This *Weltgefühl*, or apperception of the world, is called the experience of participation. Since his ego, the centre of consciousness, was still weak and unsettled, he felt also that things were fickle and not constant, and that they could change at any time in an unpredictable way. Against this feeling, too, early man reacted with magic practices to make things remain consistent and reliable or to develop in the way that he wanted.

As far as rites are concerned, they express a higher level of the evolution of consciousness. They were based on old traditional myths. Different from magical practices, ritual action can be described as the effort to affect something acausally with the help of metaphysical beings. When carrying out a rite, the celebrant—in our culture mostly called the priest—dramatised a scene of a myth in a symbolic but exactly prescribed, regulated way. It was believed that at the same moment the scene was enacted, the things reported in the myth would occur again. Unlike today's common rites, it was characteristic of the archaic conception of a rite that it was believed that by carrying out the rite, an ontological change would be achieved (e.g., the rite of the Eucharist, in which bread and wine are turned into the flesh and blood of Christ, or the Christian rite of the ordination of a priest, in which an ordinary person, a layperson, is turned into a powerful and somehow supernaturally "omnipotent" being for his or her lifetime).

Beside the belief in an acausal powerful efficacy, a certain conception of space and time was characteristic of the archaic worldview. Space, as I said before, was imagined as not yet settled and constant, but as dynamic. "Moral" qualities were even ascribed to places. That meant that people believed there were good and bad places: on the one hand, places of theophany, where good other-worldly beings chose to live, and, on the other hand, wicked and evil places where, according to Christian faith, the devil was up to mischief. Time was not yet thought to be progressing in a linear fashion, because one lived in the present, so to speak—in the very moment. Parallel to that, the observation of the seasons and of the starry sky led to the idea of time rotating in a circle. Besides, one "knew" about good and bad times, and "magicians" had the responsibility of recognising the right moment for a project. During the archaic phase, however, these beliefs were already partly overlaid with new convictions still valid today.

The evolution of consciousness during the archaic phase

The mutation of consciousness did not occur out of the blue. Although it started only with the beginning of the Modern Age, a considerable part of the evolution of consciousness had already taken place during the archaic phase. This evolution also proceeded on the metaphysical branch, through confrontation with the supernatural world and its supernatural beings, as it did on the physical branch through confrontation with the natural world here and now. Evolutionary progress, the condition for mutation, was considerably greater on the metaphysical branch than on the physical one. That is why mainly this branch is considered here. In its development, five lines can be particularly distinguished.

At first, there is a long-lasting movement that could be described as "pushing up heaven". While at the level of tribal religions, people thought the other world was attached to visible things (e.g., "holy" trees, "holy" mountains), but, by and by, people imagined the other world as further and further removed, and finally as beyond the starry firmament (see Figure 2).

During this process of "pushing up heaven", the number of metaphysical inhabitants was reduced. While there were still hosts of spirits and ghosts in the tribal religions, in the polytheistic religions there was a tendency that led from the idea of large families of gods to monotheistic conceptions of the metaphysical world.

Together with the pushing up of heaven and the reduction of other-worldly beings, a development of myths and rites took place.

Myths became less and less unsophisticated and naïve. Here is an example of a comparatively naïve myth of creation in New Zealand, which is still retold and passed on by the Maori, an ethnic group that is far retarded in evolutionary terms. This myth says that at the beginning of time, their forebear pulled their island out of the sea with a fishing rod. Then he is said to have lifted the sky so that the sun could shine on the island, but the sun ran so fast that people could not finish their work by sunset, and their forebear decided to beat the sun with a rope until it moderated its speed. This story shows how far the distance is between this primitive myth of creation and the Jewish one, for example, in which creation is brought into being out of nothing, purely through the power of words.

As to the rites, generally the idea changed as to why these rites had to be carried out. The Chortis, for example, an Indian people in Guatemala, who still practise the religion of the Maya under the surface of Christianity, dramatise their myth of creation after the winter solstice. This myth says that at the beginning of time, their god, the sun, began to rise to measure the world by her orbit throughout the year. When performing the myth of creation, the priests of the Chortis climb a "holy" mountain at a brisk pace to celebrate a "holy" meal up there

near a little "holy" lake, together with their "descended" god. Then
they very diligently select five "holy" stones on the lakeshore. Upon
returning home, they use these stones to symbolise the "holy" idol—
the "mystical" body of their "single god in five persons" in their
temple. They believe that this will have the effect of allowing the sun
to rise again after the "dismal time", and that the world, prone to fall
back into chaos, will continue to exist.

In the course of the evolution of consciousness, the performance of
certain rites was increasingly abandoned, mainly those that were
meant to secure salvation, to protect creation, to bless the fruit of agri-
culture or the outcome of wars, etc. Since then, almost the only rites
to have been performed are those believed to effect the salvation of
the soul, such as, for example, the sacramental rites of the Catholic
Church.

Concerning the mutation of consciousness, the following strand
of development is of particular importance. Together with the "pushing up of heaven", the other-worldly beings were imagined as being
less and less material. In evolutionarily primitive cultures, however, these beings were imagined as being almost of the same consis-
tence as the natural beings of this world. Through the continuous
dematerialisation of other-worldly beings, the distinction between
the material, physical world and the spiritual, metaphysical world
became increasingly evident. Matter–mind, the pair of terms resulting
from that process, seems to be one of the most important achievements of the evolution of consciousness on the basis of the archaic
worldview.

The archaic understanding of this pair of terms, though, was, at the
same time, also part of the reason for the mutation of consciousness,
since the dematerialisation of the other-worldly beings meant an
inherent structural narrowness. In addition, because the understanding of the creations of the unconscious was still concrete and not
symbolic, dematerialisation, just like a converging sequence of
numbers, tended towards an absolute limit: the notion of a "purely
immaterial, spiritual" being. However, as is known, a mathematical
sequence can never completely reach the limit it leads towards, even
if the distance between the last link of the sequence and the limit
becomes smaller and smaller, eventually becoming infinitesimal. In
the same way, the dematerialisation of the other-worldly beings,
which took place only in people's imagination, could never have been

forced so far that complete immateriality, or pure spirituality, would have been reached. An other-worldly being which so powerfully affected people's life in this world and could reveal itself to man could neither be thought of nor be imagined if it was without any substance at all.

When the movement towards the limit of a "purely spiritual" being had become infinitesimal in the wake of scholasticism, the evolution of consciousness was in danger of hitting the ceiling of this theological construction. The evolution of consciousness could only advance if a fundamentally new, no longer concrete, point of view of spirituality and mind was taken. As I said before, from that new point of view, intelligible access had to be found to the objective mind, which meant an access to the mind that had been there before, long before consciousness, the subjective mind, came into being.

Incidentally, during the Greek classical period, the evolution on the physical branch had also led to a conception of the objective mind, and that conception was concrete, too. Between 600 and 300 BC, the Greeks had learnt how to develop their abstract way of thinking. Some of their philosophers asked themselves of what kind was the existence of abstract terms. Plato and his disciple, Aristotle, conceived theories that were opposite to each other. Let us here have a look at Plato only (the question of whose conception was the right one was only thoroughly discussed in our Middle Ages).

The notions, which we define nowadays as abstracta, were called *eidoi* by Plato. This word means prefigurations, or the true origins of images. Commonly, this Greek word is translated as "ideas". Plato taught that these ideas had existed before the things themselves came into being. He thought that the ideas existed in a kind of heaven and then they would assume a definite form as "things of this world". That means he supposed the abstracta could exist on their own and that they were something concrete, albeit subtly concrete, as, later on, were the "purely spiritual beings" of scholasticism. In the history of philosophy, Plato's concept of the kind of existence of abstracta is called realism (derived from Latin *res*: a thing). For the sake of clear and unambiguous terminology, I call Plato's concept concrete: it is a concretism of philosophical notions, as distinguished from the metaphysical concretism of theologies.

So, the change in the understanding of the objective mind is the core of the mutation of consciousness, in which the archaic worldview was overcome and the epistemological foundations of religions were demolished. I should mention, at this stage of the discussion, that religious attitude was not affected or attacked by this process. Religiousness has merely changed from "religiousness *with* religion" into "religiousness *without* religion".

Before we deal with this development, we should find out how the evolutionary change of the conception of people and their world advanced. This process, too, will be only briefly outlined here.

CHAPTER TWO

The first step in the mutation of consciousness

S ince the Renaissance, intellectually open-minded people have become more and more interested in this world here and now. Efforts to explore nature and history developed into a completely new type of science which was categorically different from theology. While theology understood itself as a hermeneutic science that interpreted something that had been "revealed", the new type of science explored nature and culture empirically.

The preparatory work of scholasticism

It was about 300 years before the scholarly equipment for empirical exploration was adequately developed, but this development had already started—more or less unnoticed—before the Renaissance, when the scholastic theologians and philosophers had already done significant preparatory work, but still with a view directed towards heaven. Their work contained three important studies: the practice of logical thinking, the accomplishment of the "dispute of universalia", and the attempt—which, however, failed—to integrate Aristotle's nature study into theology. With these three projects, the scholastic faction created the absolutely necessary condition for the future development of scholarly equipment, which enabled natural scientists to make this new, empirical type of science so extraordinarily successful.

The Middle Ages brought about yet another important change of conditions, not directly for the triumph of natural sciences, but for the mutation of consciousness. This development took place rather outside the realm of scholasticism, on the political branch: the German emperors' dogged resistance against the popes' attempts to seize absolute power, worldly and political rule as well as clerical and spiritual rule. Finally, the emperors won against the popes, and when, in 1338, the Reichstag in Frankfurt under King Ludwig the Bavarian declared the so-called "Weistum of Rhense" national law, this was the basis of the future separation of state and church. Although some scholastic as well as some lay philosophers supported the emperors intellectually, the emperors alone were the ones who waged the wars, and it is astonishing that they did so in spite of the terrible weapon the popes possessed: they could anathematise people.

With the emergence of scholasticism in the eleventh century, the occidental mind somehow awoke like the sleeping beauty from a sleep that had lasted for centuries. Until then, the miserable fragments of ancient education and culture and the theology of the Fathers of the Church, which was still unsystematic, had just been passed on in a rather rough and ready way in monastery or cathedral schools. Seldom was anything new added.

Then, suddenly, the dictum *fides quaerens intellectum* emerged and spread. The essential meaning of this statement is that the contents of faith should be understood. With this dictum, for the first time, a notion or an idea appeared which, about a millennium later, led to the so-called dilemma between reason and faith. Furthermore, by overcoming and transcending that dilemma, the final breakthrough to a new worldview became possible. The notion that I have in mind is the term "reason", a word mentioned just a few lines above, because I think "reason" corresponds to the very meaning of the Latin word *intellectus*.

The appeal to use reason in order to understand and to interpret the contents of Christian faith was just a tiny germ in those days, a mere inkling of the development that later was to occur as the mutation of consciousness. For the time being, the archaic worldview was still so fixed in people's minds that during the time of scholasticism there was only a kind of intellectual preparation for the new ideas to come. Thus, it is understandable that this process was hardly noticed by most of the people. None the less, as weak as this process seems to be when we look at it nowadays, the effect must not be underestimated.

The first effect that became obvious when people started to follow the dictum *fides quaerens intellectum* was that they started to apply Aristotle's logic to the contents of Christian faith. This happened because, out of Aristotle's complete works, only his studies on logic—or dialectics, as it was called in those days—had been passed on directly to the occident: these studies had been included in the "seven free arts" which contained the fragmentary "worldly knowledge" called philosophy. During the "dark" Middle Ages, the subject "philosophy" consisted of nothing but Aristotle's logic. Until the eleventh century, its rules had merely been obstinately memorised in the monastery or cathedral schools. However, the moment that the call was heard for the application of reason to the contents of Christian faith, the explosiveness hidden in the Aristotelian dialectic quickly became obvious.

Berengar of Tours (990–1088) was the first to be really serious about confronting Christian faith with Aristotle's logic when he presented his criticism of the doctrine of the Eucharist. He said it was illogical to maintain that bread and wine were transformed or transubstantiated into Christ's body and blood if they still looked the same as before the consecration. In the language of scholasticism, that means to suppose a change of substance, although the outward appearance stays the same. Naturally, Berengar was forced to revoke his logical conclusion, but he resisted for twenty years. Only when the Easter Synod in 1079 threatened to anathematise him and to abandon him to the rage of the mob did he comply (and for the rest of his life he regretted this).

Nevertheless, the zest to apply Aristotelian logic had emerged and could not be ignored during the following centuries. At the recently founded universities, people—as if in a delirium—practised and studied logical reasoning as well as trying to discover fallacies of logic. While thinking had been turning in circles until that time, moving around its object, from that time onwards, teachers and scholars strove to learn deductive reasoning.

The second preparatory step that was necessary to accomplish the development of empirical science was taken by the theologians and philosophers when they carried out the so-called "dispute of univer-salia". In those days, "universalia" was the name for general abstract terms. The scholastic dispute about them sought to find an answer to a question that had not been found in ancient times. Probably this question had not really been of interest to ancient thinkers, but sud-denly, during the time of scholasticism, it became an urgent topic. The question was: can the mode of existence of general abstract terms adequately and correctly be explained by following Plato's ideas or Aristotle's theory? In contrast to Plato, Aristotle taught that abstracta could not exist alone, separated from our real world, and he stated that they were inside the things they were abstracted from as well as in our minds. To people nowadays, this concept seems to be natural and self-evident, but that was not the case for scholars of that time, because the Fathers of the church had favoured Plato when looking for a synthesis of Christian myth and Greek philosophy. For the early dogmatists, this was the only acceptable approach, because Plato's concretism of terms was founded, like their own thinking, on a con-crete worldview.

Indeed, the "dispute of universalia" could not be resolved in the Middle Ages, but the Franciscan William Occam (*ca* 1280–1347) sug-gested a compromise. He said that Plato's conception of the world of ideas was still true for the exploration of metaphysical nature, whereas Aristotle's theory, the so-called nominalism, or conceptualism, could be accepted for the exploration of this world's nature (which was, in any case, considered inferior in those days). With this point of view, Occam had initiated a development that determined the way of think-ing until the end of the nineteenth century. On the one hand, this compromise allowed the theologians to stick to their archaic way of thinking and, on the other hand, it gave the scientists, who strove for new empirical methods, the freedom they needed to explore that dimension of reality which archaic people had called nature in contrast to the supernatural: in other words, the new scientists could under-stand and explore nature and culture in the way we do today.

Now, the third step the scholastics worked towards was focused on their efforts to integrate Aristotle's studies on nature into Christian theology. The Aristotelian scriptures, which contained the study of nature, only became known in the occident at the time when scholas-ticism started to develop. The scriptures had survived in the Byzan-tine Empire, which stretched from Asia Minor to Gibraltar until the attack by the Arabs. The Muslims had adopted them, but the effort of the so-called Mutazilites to integrate Aristotle's thoughts into their religion had already, in the eleventh century, been suppressed by the majority of the Ulemas. In the meantime, Aristotelian scriptures were translated into Latin and commented on in Sicily and in Spain. From there, they were passed on to spiritual and intellectual centres of the occident: Paris, Oxford, and Cologne. There, it was mainly the systematic philosopher and theologian, St Thomas Aquinas, who took great pains to integrate Aristotle's thoughts—including those on nature—into Christian theology. His efforts were doomed to failure, as were the efforts of theologians to monopolise depth psychology from their point of view. In spite of the failure of such efforts in the Middle Ages, the interest in exploring nature grew. This is underlined by the fact that Occam thought it necessary to find a compromise for initiating the development, as mentioned previously. Another indication of this interest in nature resides in the Franciscan Roger Bacon (1214–1292): he was not only interested in nature, he also advocated experiments, carried out some himself, and built optical instruments, for example. However, it must be admitted that there were still quite abstruse mythical "theories" underlying his view of nature.

A new apparatus of intellectual and scientific instruments

Let us talk again about the Renaissance and early Modern Age. While theology continued to follow its archaic track and the Catholic church entered into cruel religious wars against the newly risen Protestant churches, the empirical sciences grew more or less unnoticed. According to archaic man's separation of nature from the supernatural, the science of nature as we understand it today developed independently. It branched into the science of nature and the science of culture. Both tried to proceed empirically, but this meant different things to each of them: to the historical sciences that had emerged first, it mainly meant commenting on historical sources. One result was that the model of history as the history of salvation—still valid in those days—was overturned.

To foster scientific exploration, several achievements of the mutation of consciousness were integrated into a whole. During the following centuries, this body of new intellectual and scientific instruments

allowed scientists slowly to get behind the façade of sensory perception: concerning space, that meant the exploration of the atomic
sphere of our microcosms as well as of the immense vastness of our
universal macrocosm; concerning time, it meant going back to the
beginnings of mankind and even of man's universe to find out about
man's history and the development of the universe.

To reach this goal, many more scientific results had to be added to
those achieved by scholasticism. First, it was important to learn correct observation: to count, to measure, to weigh exactly. Again, this
and the performance of experiments led to more inventions of instruments and indirectly to other new methods. One important method
that had to be learnt was the correct, exact analysis of causal connec-
tions. More than 1,500 years before that time, the pre-Socratics had
already worked on such an analysis when they categorically stated
that they no longer wanted to deal with tales about gods and god-
desses, the "mythoi", but with "ta onta", real things. But, as they
asked for the first cause of everything, from the beginning, they very
soon arrived at divine ideas and dimensions. Thus, their striving for
empirical exploration turned into natural theology. When interest in
the empirical approach arose again at the beginning of the Modern
Age, this aberration was avoided by, in principle, asking for only the
closest preceding cause, that is, by asking only for the immediate
cause for the phenomenon observed. This attitude made it possible,
for the first time in history, to probe step by step behind the façade of
outer appearance and sensuous illusion. In addition, one had to work
out an empirically based theory—no longer a mythical one—in which
all the various phenomena observed could systematically be
explained. Moreover, a new attitude towards this new theory had to
be found, which resulted in the principle of methodical doubt. That
meant that a scientist should be ready to abandon a theory he or she
favoured as soon as this theory no longer explained the phenomena
observed, or was incompatible with the facts observed. A new and
more differentiated theory had to replace the old one. Such new theories were not only an affirmation of the facts stated, they were also of
heuristic importance. By raising new questions, these theories initiated more aim-orientated research. The step of replacing theories
which were no longer adequate with more differentiated ones had
already been established by Occam's compromise in his time, when
he accepted Aristotle's worldview for the exploration of this world

here and now. That meant that people's thinking no longer had to turn in circles around mental or spiritual "things" which stayed the same forever in a heaven of ideas. In contrast to that way of thinking, the new approach implied an immense dynamic.

All these elements of empirical research were integrated into the unique apparatus I mentioned above, an apparatus of intellectual and scientific instruments never heard of before.

However, this was a strenuous and difficult process of finding out and testing. Only in the eighteenth century was this development more or less completed. In the course of these efforts, nature studies became natural sciences and historiography became the science of history.

All the new things that could be detected with the newly worked out methods and instruments cannot be enumerated here, but the amount and quality is of unique importance in human history. The results can be looked up in any book dealing with the history of sciences, but it seems to me important to keep in mind that—in contrast to most people's opinion—it was not the philosophers who changed our view of the world, but the extraordinarily great number of empirically based discoveries. Interestingly enough, scientists hardly thought about the consequences of their discoveries for our view of the world. The people who did so were the philosophers, albeit with hindsight.

The Age of Enlightenment

Now we have already reached the Age of Enlightenment. Usually, it is identified with the eighteenth century. This century is characterised by the fact that alert minds reflected on the consequences for the archaic view of the world of discoveries achieved through historical and scientific research. With hindsight, one called the possessors of such minds philosophers. The French philosophers were the philosophers of the Enlightenment who saw things most distinctly and intelligibly. Then a certain number of British philosophers supported that new attitude, too, whereas the number of German philosophers was the smallest. It must be said, though, that the scientist who was most important for the mutation of consciousness was a German who lived in Paris. His name was Baron Paul von Holbach.

He and the others were no longer the "great, lonesome thinkers" of the past because, during the time of absolutism, something had developed that we now call "the public": a mainly bourgeois society that discussed all the problems that hitherto had been exclusively topics of the nobility and the church. The discussions took place in the salons, in art exhibitions, and in the foyers of theatres, and, in spite of the strict censorship carried out by the state in co-operation with the church, many progressive papers and books proclaiming the ideas of the Enlightenment were distributed. The most influential book, in fact the classic work of the Enlightenment, was an encyclopaedia conceived and written by a team of authors. One member of the team was Paul von Holbach. Instead of the sociological term "public", one could also use the expression "public opinion". In any case, it was new that the "common people" could now have their own opinions and that they dared to express them. In this public sphere, the spirit of the Enlightenment emerged.

The political and ideological strand of the Enlightenment

If one talks about the Enlightenment, one should distinguish between two strands: the political and the ideological. The political strand was essentially a continuation of a process that had been initiated in the Middle Ages by the struggle between papacy and empire. While, in those times, the principalities gained their independence from the popes, in the eighteenth century subjects fought for their rights against the principality, at least mentally and verbally. They claimed the idea of the sovereignty of the people and wanted democracy as well as legal security. In these ideas, a facet of that development which I call the mutation of consciousness becomes obvious.

The ideological strand led to people's new understanding of themselves and of their world. To understand it not only in its importance and singularity, but also in its narrowness, one has first to consider the notion of empiricism: in the sciences, it was the only accepted approach to perceivable things in those days.

In the archaic worldview, there was still the distinction between seeing with the eyes of your body and seeing with the eyes of your soul. Seeing with the eyes and hearing with the ears of your body meant, for archaic people, the same as sensory perception means to us nowadays. Seeing with the eyes of the soul meant our perception of reality in dreams and visions. Since the discovery of the unconscious, this process is called inner perception, and means the information that flows from the self to the ego. While the ego is the centre of consciousness, the self is the centre of the unconscious and, simultaneously, of the psyche in its totality. The area of consciousness is a small part within the sphere of the unconscious. The psyche comprises both consciousness and the unconscious.

From the archaic point of view, the flow of information was interpreted quite differently. It was believed that the information came from outside, even from the other world, the supernatural one. This misunderstanding will be examined later, and we will see that this error resulted in the archaic view of understanding ourselves and our world.

However, first we have to realise how narrow was the concept of perceptible reality that formed the basis of former empirical research. One has to remember that until the end of the Age of Enlightenment—that is, until the brink of the twentieth century—that which was recognised as scientifically proved was only what had been perceived through our natural senses, or through our senses being technically enlarged, improved, and made more precise. This scientific attitude is called methodical positivism.

Nevertheless, at the beginning of empirical research, this strict reduction to sensory perceivable things was absolutely necessary. Only by carefully sticking to methodical positivism could scientists overcome the former kind of seemingly increasing knowledge which was based on speculation. Abandoning the well-liked sources out of which myths had poured and explained the world since time immemorial was a hard thing to do.

Of course, in archaic times people had asked questions concerning the origin of the world, of plants and animals, of mankind, etc., but because the cognitive means to give an empirical–scientific explanation did not exist, speculations (creations of the unconscious) filled the vacuum of knowledge. Thus, many mythical "theories" of various kinds developed: mythical cosmogonies (doctrines about the creation) and cosmologies, mythical antinomies, physiologies, and pharmacologies, mythical doctrines about the descent of man, animals, etc. Seen from today's point of view, these myths were often rather absurd. How tenacious they could and can be becomes obvious when we see how astrology persists, or how the dispute in the USA about creationism continues—not to mention the mythically expository rubbish that is disseminated by the so-called esoteric movements.

The consistent observance of methodical positivism had two effects: on the one hand, it allowed the gradual progress of penetrating the façade of sensory deception, as I mentioned before, and led to an enlargement and increase of knowledge which effected a completely new view of nature and history; on the other hand, it led to a demythologising of nature and the history of culture. This was not directly intended, because the only aim of empirical research was the increase of knowledge. However, the indirect side effect of the empirical point of view was the overcoming of mythical theories, and that brought about the blowing away of mythical fog. The expression "enlightenment" might allude to that process.

It was not only the illustrative myths that were eliminated, to be replaced by empirically based knowledge; methodical positivism changed, too, and turned into an ideological position during the Age of Enlightenment. That meant, explicitly, everything that cannot be perceived through our senses does not exist. This strict statement was aimed at archaic man's concept of the other, supernatural world and declared that it—including God—did not exist.

Consequently, the view of the world resulting from ideological positivism, which was the worldview of the Enlightenment, was atheistic. However, that was not the case right from the beginning, when most representatives of the Enlightenment were still deists. They still supposed that there was a God who had created the world, but thought that he had later abandoned it and left it to itself. Even Voltaire, who maybe most heatedly argued and represented the ideas of the Enlightenment, was still a deist. The first radically consistent atheist was Paul von Holbach, in my opinion.

Eliminatory materialism

It must be added that the worldview of the Age of Enlightenment was not only atheistic, but also materialistic in a certain way. If we look at it in the context of the mutation of consciousness, the positivistic intermediate phase had an essential function in the antithetical development of man's worldview. Let us keep in mind that the mutation of consciousness most probably occurred because the concretism of the archaic conception of the objective mind had to be overcome. The late archaic position said that the other world was ideal, spiritual, or metaphysical, whereas this world, here and now, was material or physical. Besides that, the other-worldly spirits were believed to be arbitrarily able to affect this world acausally, purely by the energy of their thinking and will. However, when empirical research proved that the process of nature followed regular patterns, the natural laws, the late archaic position was abandoned and, because ideological positivism had completely eliminated the idea of an other-worldly, supernatural world, only this natural world remained, imagined as a merely material one. It was Paul von Holbach who described the strong, far-reaching impact of this new worldview in his book *Le système de la nature*.

If one calls this worldview materialistic, as is commonly done, one should be aware of the fact that it is an eliminatory materialism, because not only the idea of mind, intellect, or spirit in general, but also the archaic conception of the objective mind was eliminated by empirical research. We shall see later what kind of basically new idea of mind, or, more exactly, of matter and mind, emerged with the second step of the mutation of consciousness.

The rationalistic conception of man

During the Age of Enlightenment, not only did the view of the world change, but also that of man: to be more precise, the idea of mind in man. In spite of very radical materialism, it was never denied that man is provided with a mind, or with a mental, intellectual, spiritual dimension. However, it is true that some people believed—especially in the first part of the twentieth century—that man's mind could gradually be reduced to the laws of physics and chemistry and be explained that way. This position was called ontological reductionism. For the moment, we will leave this topic and return to it later.

Now, let us have a look at the difference between the positivistic and archaic worldview. From the archaic point of view, man's mind was a part of the soul, provided with many capacities. It was further believed that his mind was only a weak glimmer that needed the enlightenment of the divine spirit in order that man could find his way in the world.

In the Age of Enlightenment, the phenomenon which archaic man had imagined to be his soul was reduced to reason (ratio), or to consciousness, as we would call it today. Reason was seen as a great light that enabled man to illuminate the last dark and unknown corners of reality and to understand the meaning of good and bad. Today, this overestimation of man's reason is called rationalism and, according to this attitude, the conception of man in the Age of Enlightenment is called rationalistic, whereas the conception of the world is called positivistic–materialistic.

The dilemma between knowledge and faith

Because the archaic worldview had continued to thrive undisputed in the churches, in the Age of Enlightenment two irreconcilable worldviews faced each other. This situation was felt and expressed as the dilemma between knowledge and faith.

For a long time, it seemed to be impossible to overcome this dilemma. Innumerable discussions among experts, theologians as well as empirically researching scientists, ended without any satisfying answers. Again, the evolution of consciousness seemed to hit the ceiling of narrow theoretical models or constructions, similar to the situation at the end of scholasticism (the dispute of universalia).

It is the nature of a dilemma that its antagonistic contrasts cannot be harmonised. They have to be overcome, to be transcended. This cannot be achieved through pure reasoning; it just happens. The fact that it happens results from an insight into psychic processes of change. This insight was only possible after the discovery of the unconscious.

When accompanying processes of individuation, Jung observed that large steps in psychic change—leading from an outdated attitude to a fundamentally new one—did not happen smoothly or linearly. He became aware of the fact that, at first, a new position had to develop which was contrary to the outdated one and irreconcilable with it, and because there are arguments in favour and arguments against each of the two positions, a rationally unsolvable dilemma arises for the person concerned. If someone can stand this tension long enough, and if he does not decide too hastily for the one or the other position, merely for reasons of convenience, a solution emerges which transcends the old conflict and unifies the controversial positions on a higher level. It seems as if it happens automatically, just by itself. On the one hand, the unifying solution that emerges from the unconscious relativises each position, but, on the other hand, it saves elements of each position that remain precious, and integrates them into a new unity. Because the dilemma is transcended in this subconsciously occurring process, Jung calls it the law of antithetical tension and transcending function.

Looking back at human history, we can recognise that the phylogenetic change that I call the mutation of consciousness follows the same law as the ontogenetic change which Jung observed in processes of individuation (see Figure 1).

At the end of the Middle Ages, the dematerialisation of otherworldly beings infinitesimally approached the ultimate grade of spiritualisation of beings, and the evolution of consciousness was in danger of hitting the ceiling of theoretical and intellectual constructions, but the antithetical tension was not yet possible. The reason for that situation was that during the archaic phase, evolution had taken place almost solely on the metaphysical branch. That meant evolution on the physical branch had first to catch up with the metaphysical one. This became possible due to the fast and forceful rise of the empirical sciences, as mentioned previously. Their new positivistic position became the antipodes to the archaic view and led to the antithetical tension expressed in the "dilemma between knowledge and faith", a tension that was necessary for the further advancement of the evolution of consciousness.

When this tension had become extremely strong, the dilemma was transcended. Again, it was not overcome by pure reasoning and rational insight, as does not happen in the processes of individuation, either. Transcending just happened as the result of empirically based discoveries. The fact that these discoveries had helped to transcend the dilemma and to initiate a new view of man and man's world became visible only some decades later, again as a result of philosophical reflection. This process happened through a new kind of philosophising suited to modern times: through interdisciplinary fundamental research in human sciences. The decisive step in this process was the insight that the discoveries mentioned before had widened the notion of empiricism.

The shadow of the positivistic–materialistic worldview

That meant that the positivistic–materialistic worldview was only a preliminary worldview: a necessary transient phase which had the function of creating the antithetical tension needed for the break-through to a new view of man and his world.

However, there was a price to be paid for the one-sidedness of the ideological positivism which excluded everything people had received through their faith in a supernatural world in former times. People did not have access to an old familiar source any longer, neither to the source of meaning nor to that of ethical norms and true spirituality.

First, let us look at the consequences for ethical norms. Ethical norms, or laws, in archaic cultures were considered to be objectively founded because archaic people believed these norms were revealed to human beings from heaven. On the one hand, heaven as a concrete, other-worldly reality has turned out to be an illusion, but, on the other hand, nowadays we also know from Freud's and Jung's discoveries that the phenomena which archaic people believed to be supernatural "things" or messages revealed to man are creations of the unconscious which the ego receives by inner perception. As the unconscious is part of the objective psychical, one can again say that ethics were objectively founded in the archaic world, too. Yet another phenomenon can be explained by Jung's view of the psyche. It explains the astonishing fact that all known ethical systems have proved to be merely variations of one fundamental pattern, in spite of all the differences that have become visible in comparative studies of various cultures. In the light of human ethology, one can say that this fundamental pattern is, like many other things, an expression of an ethogram that is typical of homo sapiens.

Against this background, let us find out how a source of ethical norms was conceived from the positivistic point of view. As I said before, it was not only believed that human reason (ratio) was the only mental or spiritual reality in the world, but it was also said that through reason man was able to distinguish between good and bad and to recognise which way of acting was right or wrong. What the philosophy of the Enlightenment called reason, we call consciousness nowadays. According to the model of human psyche as it developed after the discovery of the unconscious, consciousness is attributed to the subjective psychical, different from the unconscious, which is attributed to the objective psychical. So, the conception of man in the Age of Enlightenment resulted in subjectively founded ethics.

This is not only an academic question, as becomes obvious in today's widespread regret about the loss of values and guidelines for our way of acting. As we shall see in our discussion later on, mature conscious decisions are the result of optimising the relation between the aspirations of the unconscious and the ambitions of our consciousness. Furthermore, it has to be kept in mind that in this process our consciousness is ultimately subordinate to the unconscious, even though consciousness has a considerable range of freedom. In the language of cybernetics, one could say that consciousness as a subsystem is linked to the unconscious in such a way that it receives steady feedback from it which it can rely on. Therefore, it is guaranteed that conscious decisions do not stray too far beyond the limits set by the typical pattern.

Nevertheless, the feedback from the unconscious was no longer listened to and became lost in the subjectively founded ethics of the Enlightenment. Hence, the floodgates were opened to arbitrariness, and the highest value— given by nature and stored in man's ethogram—had become lost. Everybody could adopt his or her own private, subjective, self-made worldview. Through this so-called ideologisation of one's worldview, a certain fragmentary truth was dogmatised. This "truth" was declared to be the highest value that decided what was right and what was wrong.

As long as the *anciens règimes*, which had been based on the alliance of throne and altar, were still in power, the ideologising of the value system was limited to the private sphere. In public, the old, traditional, Christian–humanistic values were still accepted as before and the state laws were in accordance with these values.

How disastrous the effect of subjective ethics can be, after the loss of objective values, people had to experience in the twentieth century, when ideologies such as Communism and National Socialism seized control over state power.

In Germany, for example, this was painfully experienced, when Hitler succeeded in seizing power and in eliminating the valid constitution. Thus, he was able to enforce a value system in Germany by means of violence, a system which he worked out in the context of the ideology he had tinkered with during his time in Vienna. As the

purity of the Aryan race was one of the highest values in this ideology, it seemed to be justifiable and right to Hitler and his followers to
extinguish and kill everybody and everything that sullied this race,
according to their opinion with regard to their ideology: the Jews, the
gypsies, the people suffering from hereditary disease and insanity,
and homosexuals became their victims. In addition, because the Nazis
considered the Aryan race to be a superior "master race", it seemed to
be right to them to enslave the Slavic "sub-people". In analogy, this
is true of Soviet Communism, too. Based on the ideology that was
valid in the Soviet Union, it was officially proclaimed to be right to
eliminate "the enemy of the working class".

In both cases, the people in power seemed to believe that they
could follow the intrinsic logic of their value system and, convinced
that they were doing the right thing, maintain a clear conscience. That
might sound cynical, but, depressingly, these examples show how
disastrous the effects of subjective ethics can be.

National Socialism and Soviet Communism were fortunately
overcome and abolished. In Germany, the fathers of the German
Constitution aligned themselves once again with the traditional
Christian–humanistic values. I believe that was the correct thing to
do in those days. However, today, some concrete Christian concepts
derived from examples in the bible sometimes turn out to be stum-
bling blocks in the path of an urgently needed adaptation of ethics to
meet the demands of sciences and technology, which have rapidly
advanced in the meantime.

These new questions become obvious when we look at the efforts
on various levels to establish guidelines for the handling of embryo
cells, for artificial fertilisation, for abortion, and for medically assisted
suicide. There are also new questions when looking at the needs and
denied rights of immigrants and socially disadvantaged people in our
modern societies.

While, in the political sphere, the traditional fundamental values
have more or less been restored, in social life the positivistic worldview and, resulting from it, subjective ethics have spread more and
more, whereas Christianity seems to have evaporated. Hence, an arbi-
trary system has emerged in which certain values, such as power, a
good income, sexuality, consumption, or just fun are the highest
values that determine an individual's way of acting. This seems to be
the cause of the frightening disintegration of tradition and ethics

which is happening in front of our eyes and which makes our culture appear detestable in, for example, the view of Muslims. In fact, because of the incredibly fast changes in civilisation and society, the adaptation of ethics should have been—and still should be—very urgent, but it should be within the ethogram typical of man, because it must be considered that the positivistic worldview and its inherent subjective ethics have spread extensively only in the past two centuries. In the Age of Enlightenment, this view was still restricted to a few.

The awareness that now the positivistic worldview has reached and deeply influenced the large majority of the European population—although many people are still believed to be Christians—is reason enough to consider more intensely how the new worldview has developed. Interestingly enough, this new view gave people another chance to work out objectively founded ethics. This was and is possible through the discoveries of depth psychology, the new type of empirical science, which emerged at the end of the twentieth century.

CHAPTER THREE

The second step in the mutation of consciousness

*Transcending the dilemma of knowledge and faith
in two branches of research*

At the beginning of the twentieth century, the dilemma between knowledge and faith was transcended, even though only *de facto*. This meant that the decisive second step of the mutation of consciousness had been initiated. Transcending had, *de facto*, been caused by empirically founded discoveries, as I said before. These discoveries had been achieved in two separate branches of research independently of each other: first, in the branch that has led to today's group of the sciences of cognition, and second, in the branch of the traditional natural sciences. First, the breakthrough occurred in the branch of the cognitive strand when the unconscious was empirically proved. The main effect of this proof was a new view of man. Later, a new view of the world emerged through new discoveries in physics and biology. However, these processes only happened *de facto*, for the time being, and the fact that materialism had been overcome through these new discoveries would be realised only later.

At the same time, when a new self-understanding and a new understanding of the world was being worked out, the "resurrection of the objective mind in a new form" took place. This was, as far as I can see, the meaning of the mutation of consciousness. In the 1970s, it became possible to recognise that the archaic concrete conception of mind, which, at the end of the Middle Ages, had caused danger of stagnancy in the evolution of consciousness because of being limited by its old, narrow, theoretical framework, was finally overcome by empirical research in the following centuries. The essential point of this change was the insight that it was no longer necessary to distinguish between matter and mind, but only between the material and the mental aspects of an essentially holistic spatio–temporal entity according to the complementary thinking that had been developed in the meantime. I will go into detail later.

Mental streams in the nineteenth century that paved the way for something new

The decisive discoveries did not happen out of the blue. Like the discoveries that caused the first step of the evolution of consciousness, these discoveries were preceded by mental preparations, too. It happened at a time when the positivistic worldview had reached its peak, and its incompatibility with the still persisting archaic one caused painful tension in more and more people.

At least six mental streams can be distinguished which prepared the transcending of the dilemma without directly intending to do so. First, there was romanticism, with its tendency towards irrationalism, emotion, and fantasy, and second, there was the philosophy of German idealism with its unrealistic conception of mind. Furthermore, there was the influence of neo-gnosis, ethnology, and religious studies. Even within the churches, "softening" movements could be detected: in the Protestant church, liberal theology emerged, and in the Catholic church the effort to enunciate new dogmas about the Virgin Mary was noteworthy. I shall comment on only two of them shortly: on the gnosis and on the dogmas about the Virgin Mary.

The dogmas missed their aim. I think this was because of the papal church, the strong hierarchical structure of which maintained a strict orthodoxy. Nevertheless, concerning the latent effect of the evolutionary tendency, the mere fact that these dogmas were proclaimed is remarkable, because dogmas can be understood as creations of the unconscious. This discovery contributed a great deal to the second step of the mutation of consciousness. The collective unconscious provides impulses of correction against one-sided attitudes of the spirit of the age, the *Zeitgeist*, through dogmas, for example. However, it is possible that the message of the dogmas does not reach their own authors because it goes beyond their grasp. The attitude that was meant to be corrected by these dogmas about the Virgin Mary was the extremely one-sided rationalism, which also became increasingly manifest in cultural and intellectual life outside of sciences.

Four dogmas had been prepared at that time: Maria Immaculata (Mary immaculate, free from original sin), Mediatrix (mediator of grace, Mary as a mediator between people and Jesus Christ), Co-redemptrix (co-redeemer), and Assumpta (Mary's bodily assumption into heaven). In these dogmas, a Sophia figure was created in the language of the unconscious. This figure symbolises feminine (*anima*) mentality in contrast to masculine (*animus*) mentality, as is illustrated in the *logos* (reason, rationality). In using these expressions, Jung does not intend to define what is typical of men's way of thinking in comparison to that of women, but perhaps we could say that the "*anima* attitude" seems to be more common in women than in men.

The gender of imaginary figures can be used in the language of the unconscious as a symbol for circumstances that can hardly be described verbally. While the *animus* way of thinking is orientated towards gaining factual knowledge, towards distinguishing and analysing as well as towards representational formulations, the *anima* way of thinking is inclined towards being holistic, towards experiencing, participating in experiences, and towards compassion: an attitude of mind that appreciates relatedness and relationships to people and things more than the knowledge about their being the way they are. With the dogma about the Co-redemptrix, the unconscious pointed to the fact that it was not a question of replacing the *logos* attitude with a "Sophia attitude", but only of one complementing the other. The Roman Catholic church—at least, its hierarchy—did not understand this providential message inherent in these dogmas. The message deteriorated into a Marian piety that showed contempt for the body and adored virginal immaculateness.

Of all the preparatory streams outside the church, neo-gnosis is to be considered first because its way of thinking somehow anticipated the new conception of man. Gnosis is a type of religion that developed mainly in India. Because of the different kind of creation myths inherent in it, it varies from the theistic type of religion which is represented by the Jews, the Christians, and the Muslims. In contrast to the theistic religions, which believe in a personal creator who deliberately created the world, in gnostic religions, people believe that at the beginning of time there was impersonal "divine abundance" (pleroma). Out of this divine substance, a part emanated as substance pours out of a brimming pot. During this process, various spheres, inhabited by different types of spirits, emerged. The last being that came into existence, shortly before the substance became cold, was man. Even though he was afflicted with wicked and non-spiritual matter, he still carried a residue of divine substance in himself. According to the gnostic view, through spiritual efforts he could heat up this residue and approach the pleroma again. It was believed one would gain gnosis in this way. In this context, therefore, gnosis should be translated as "consciousness".

In the nineteenth century, there was a wave of exoticism and gnostic thoughts coming from India which flooded Europe. The best-known development of this so-called theosophy is the anthroposophy founded by Rudolf Steiner. The novelty and the forward-looking aspect of this gnostic stream is: whereas, in theistic religions, God and man are radically different and man is completely dependent on divine grace, according to gnostic faith man can again come closer to the divine through his own efforts. Later, we will see that the gnostic mythical view of man found an analogue in the then empirically based model of depth psychology.

Depth psychology

The emergence of a new, empirical type of psychology

The strand of research that has finally led to today's group of sciences of cognition started with the emergence of an empirical psychology. Psychology had already existed, of course, since the various beginnings of culture, but it was still mythic. Although a vast amount of well-observed phenomena was worked upon, its theoretical evaluation still happened according to the archaic worldview, which understood the soul as a spiritual being capable of an existence of its own.

Within this conception, the ideas of the soul and parts of the soul differed considerably, depending on culture and the degree of the evolution of consciousness.

Empirical psychology did not develop before the middle of the nineteenth century. It was one of the last big branch-offs from the tree of the empirical sciences: after physics, astronomy, chemistry, geo-sciences, and biology. Because this new type of psychology was based on such a solid and empirically approved foundation, within half a century of its emergence it succeeded in transcending the dilemma between knowledge and faith. The psychology of consciousness marked the beginning of this process.

The young psychological discipline needed those fifty years, because it had emerged still under the influence of the positivistic worldview. From this point of view, psyche and consciousness were considered to be the same, as I said before, and so the psychology of the early decades was a psychology of consciousness. Although it mostly analysed processes of perception, which means processes that mainly happen unconsciously, it still used the paradigm of conscious-ness as its model of explanation.

For a long time, philosophers such as, for example, Schelling, Eduard von Hartmann, and the physician and philosopher Gustav Carus, had postulated an unconscious area of the psyche. Later, empirical scientists also posited such an area or dimension. In the latter group, two lines can be distinguished: one in the field of neuro-biology, and the other in the field of psychology.

In the UK, the physiologist, Benjamin Carpenter, and the physi-cian, Thomas Laycock, discovered during the analysis of the so-called voluntary movements that the neurological function of the brain was not limited to conscious and voluntary actions, but that it comprised a wide spectrum of involuntary functions. Both scientists explicitly spoke of an unconscious cerebration and postulated the existence of a spontaneous or involuntary ego.

In the field of psychology, the American, William James, and the Frenchman, Martin Charcot, in particular, postulated an unconscious area, a sphere of the psyche. James concluded this from his observa-tions and the analysis of conversions in the context of Free Church revivalist movements and Charcot posited such a model of the psyche because of his experiences and efforts when treating so-called mental illnesses. The idea of the unconscious was in the air. Nevertheless, a method to prove the existence of the unconscious in a scientifically empirical way was still missing.

The discovery of the unconscious in 1900

It was Freud (1856–1939) who provided the empirical proof of the existence of the unconscious and founded the psychology of the unconscious. Through the facts and data that have been discovered in this field of research, the archaic as well as the positivistic worldview has been overcome.

The psychology of the unconscious is generally known today through its application in psychotherapeutic schools such as those of psychoanalysis, analytical psychology, and many others. However, the theoretical background to these schools is known to only a few. One reason is that it was only recently that it was structured and systematised. As I believe that the fact that outdated worldviews have been overcome can only be comprehended by knowing the background of this development, this chapter deals comparatively extensively with the psychology of the unconscious.

Let us start with the founder of this new method of research. Freud's method consisted of freely associating and of analysing dreams, and in these ways he succeeded in making people recollect things that had disappeared from their consciousness and had become unconscious.

Despite the fact that dreams had been generally ignored and neglected because of the view that "Dreams are but shadows", or "Dreams are ten a penny", Freud took them seriously. This proved to be an ingenious idea, which resulted in enormous effects on psychology as well as on our understanding of ourselves and our world. The analysis of dreams provided proof of the existence of the unconscious and, at the same time, provided the opportunity to explore that area of the psyche which is not directly accessible to our consciousness. Very early on, Freud believed that the dream is the *via regiae*, the ideal way, to our unconscious, but it still took some time for the methodical instruments used by Freud to become fully and effectively developed.

Freud's studies also had an effect that has relatively rarely been considered by people: in principle, he overcame ideological positivism and also the dichotomy between knowledge and faith simply by applying his method. Through the proof that dreams are not *created* by our egos, as had been taught until Freud's time, but that dreams are *perceived* by the ego, it has become evident that there is a perception, different from outward perception, that runs through our senses to our consciousness. This perception that was newly discovered then is now called inner perception. Thus, it can be distinguished terminologically from sensual perception, including that of the vegetative system, and the six somatic senses and telepathy. So, Freud theoretically enlarged the notion of empiricism that had been valid until that time, and founded a new type of empirical science. However, it seems that he himself never fully realised what theoretical effect his observations and studies had on *Weltanschauungen* and sciences. Freud remained a positivist until the end of his life. That was possibly the reason that he could not tolerate Jung's discoveries. There is still another reason, which I shall discuss later.

The breakthrough that was achieved with Freud's proof that dreams are perceived by the ego has been further enlarged and reinforced since Jung (1875–1961) explored visions and provided evidence that visions are a kind of dreams, though not received by the ego while it is sleeping, but while it is awake and faced with conditions of its consciousness. Later, I shall return to the subject of visions, because an understanding of them is indispensable for comprehending and discussing the archaic worldview and theology.

Because the inner perceptions are semantically and syntactically formed texts coded in metaphorical language, depth psychology subsumes daydreams, dreams, and visions under the general term "creations of the unconscious".

Scientists often called Jung a fantasist. Yet, again and again, he pointed out in discussions with them that he had made his discoveries empirically. Nevertheless, he could never say exactly in what way the empiricism he used differed from the empiricism of positivistic sciences. In fact, this difference could not be clearly defined before the 1970s, when an interdisciplinary group of scientists worked on establishing a new view of man by providing and discussing different approaches, methods, experiences, prejudices, aims, and hopes. In the necessary discourses, the scientific status of depth psychology was often denied by positivists as well as by theologians; thus, the Jungian psychologists especially were forced to catch up with the theoretical reflection of their own approach, something that had been neglected by Jung and his school until then. That also meant a reflection on the epistemological foundations of depth psychology.

Two phases of the discovery of the unconscious

More than a decade after Freud had provided empirical evidence of the unconscious, it became obvious that through this method (i.e., his understanding of dreams) only a superficial "layer" of the unconscious could be explored, which meant that what could be explored were only those contents that a person had once been conscious of, but which had been repressed from his consciousness because of its incompatibility with the "common ruling opinion".

The exploration of further areas of the unconscious resulted from hard striving for an understanding of the so-called archaic residues in dreams: these remains are elements with which the dreamer cannot associate anything from his personal life history. These elements deal with figures whose existence cannot be verified in the world we perceive, such as water sprites, centaurs, angels, demons, and gods. They also deal with processes or events which contradict the natural laws of physics and human logical thinking, such as, for example, the statement that God acausally fertilises a human virgin who later bears a divine child, and that a man lights a fire at the bottom of the sea, or that a dead person comes back to life again.

It is this discussion about the meaning of such contents of dreams that took place between Freud and Jung in 1909. In that year they went together on a lecture trip through the USA for seven weeks, and during that time they intensively interpreted each other's dreams. Freud strongly maintained that those so-called remains were meaningless relics from former phases of human development. Jung, however, came more and more to believe that it was precisely these figures and motifs that contained the most important information about the unconscious. Because of this fundamental difference of opinion, the two scientists eventually separated and went their different ways.

After their journey in the USA, Jung started to work on his theory in order to provide scientific evidence to support his thesis, at first without having any inkling of the approaching separation from Freud. Unlike Freud, Jung had a wide knowledge of mythology, and he was struck by the fact that the "archaic remains" in dreams consisted of the same processes and figures that appear in myths. From that, he concluded that myths, as well as dreams, are creations of the unconscious: they are originally inwardly perceived metaphorical illustrations of facts and relationships, mainly psychic ones. They cannot be described in the way we describe our sensually perceived world.

In order to understand the "archaic" images and sequences of images, Jung took a similar path to that of comparative linguistics when comparing the myths of various cultures whose meaning had often already been explored by theological or other studies and reflections. In this way, Jung recognised that the immense variety of figures and events could be reduced to few essential patterns in human life, to topics such as: lavishing care and attention, exploring the unknown, dangerous world, the transition from an outdated attitude to a more advanced one, etc. He called such categories of meaning "archetypes". The three categories just mentioned above were known as the archetype of the anima, of the hero, and of transition.

From his long and intensive observation of myths of all times and places, as well as dreams in which always the same patterns of meanings—the archetypes—appeared, Jung concluded that these patterns were specific to the species homo sapiens. That means, in today's language, that these patterns are phylogenetically acquired. This conclusion led to one that posits that there are central cerebral structures, rather like software, which produce images that correspond to these patterns. Unfortunately, Jung was somewhat careless with his terminology, calling these structures archetypes as well. This has led to much confusion.

Jung later said that the term "archetype" was the key he had needed to explore the myths as well as the unconscious. It was an insight that effected various developments, not only in mythology and depth psychology, but also in some sciences of culture. For traditional archaic theology, the consequences were deadly.

Let us return to the creations of the unconscious: they are not simple images strung together one after another, but instead are structured like the words of a text. So, out of an amount of synonymous images that can illustrate a situation, a specific one is selected that fits the concrete context.

Furthermore, in a completely recollected dream, a characteristic structure can be noticed and described. As in a Greek drama, one can distinguish four phases: exposition, complication, crisis, and solution. Around 1920, all these discoveries made Jung believe that there were not only single archetypes (of the second meaning) in the unconscious, but also a central authority producing language as well as a neuronal structure as its basis.

His supposition, that there was a spontaneously active "authority" capable of integrating, was confirmed by long-term observations of processes of development which he called processes of individuation. He had noticed that these processes occurred in such a way as if from the unconscious somebody was organising and directing the processes and urging the ego to develop. Furthermore, it struck him that individuation processes followed a typical pattern in spite of all individual variations of the course of development. It seemed as if the same fixed sequence of phases, with certain embedded tasks, had to be passed successfully. That meant that in the central leading authority—the self—a phylogenetic programme for the ontogenesis of consciousness was stored.

A paradigm shift

For psychology as a science, the empirical evidence of the unconscious meant a change of paradigm in the way Thomas Kuhn introduced the term into the theory of sciences. Thus, depth psychology developed out of the psychology of consciousness and was founded—as mentioned previously—on the new understanding of empiricism enlarged by the sphere of inner perception. Usually, changes of paradigm establish themselves within one generation, but that was not the case with empirical psychology. In fact, academic psychology is still dominant at universities today, and continues to be positivistic. One reason for this development might be that academic psychology once emerged from physiology, which means from the physical examination of healthy people, whereas the discovery of the unconscious occurred in the field of medicine when physicians tried to heal psychic anomaly or disturbances. This and other developments might help to explain why there are two completely different types of empirical psychology today. Early empirical psychology, for example, joined the philosophical departments that were strongly influenced by positivism and who hardly realised what kind of progress had occurred in medical research. This lack of communication was common at universities, because faculties mentally isolated themselves from each other.

The deeper reason for the peculiarity of the existence of two types of empirical psychology, however, is the discovery of the unconscious, which brought about a new view and conception of man, as we shall see later. The difficulty is that an individual's step from an old-fashioned view of man to a fundamentally new one is not just an act of receiving information but, rather, an act of becoming conscious of something. Such a process, however, follows its own rules. First of all, usually there is severe psychic resistance, because following and realising a phylogenetic step to a new degree of consciousness is exhausting, and often demands a painstaking, arduous, mental confrontation.

Depth psychology: a new type of empirical science

Finally, we still have to find out why depth psychology is not just a new branch of the tree of empirical sciences but, indeed, is a completely new type of empirical science.

Let us look at the inner structure of empirical sciences (Figure 3). At first, we have to keep in mind that we have to distinguish between a practical and a scientific field.

Practical depth psychology has two functions. On the one hand, it is meant to be a therapy to cure psychic disorder and it might lead to the supervision of an individuation process. Accompanying such a process is no longer called psychotherapy, but psychagogics. On the other hand, practical depth psychology also means the collecting of data in the same way as empirical sciences.

In order to understand what the collecting of data means in the case of depth psychology, we have to enquire into its typical method, because it is not possible simply to sit down with the analysand and to interpret his/her dreams. First, it is necessary to find out what kind of problem the client is facing. In contrast to an educator's approach, it is a generally accepted fundamental approach of analysts that they do not believe that they know what is the correct solution for the client. They suppose that the client's unconscious knows the answer.

So, the therapist observes how the unconscious reacts to the present situation of the person's consciousness and observes what

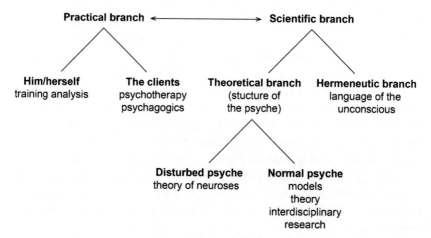

Figure 3. The structure of depth psychology.

kind of images, imagination, dreams, and even visions the client experiences or remembers. Then, the therapist tries to understand these messages. That means depth psychology focuses on the mutual exchange between consciousness and the unconscious. From the observations gained in this way, depth psychology tries to develop the theoretical models of the functions of the psyche in the same way as empirical scientific theories.

This approach of depth psychology differs in several ways from that of the psychology of consciousness. While the latter works with ordinary persons, depth psychology is primarily concerned with the support of people who suffer from psychic irritations. The psychology of consciousness proceeds actively, following its concept of the psyche by using experiments, tests, and questionnaires, whereas a depth psychologist has to remain passive at first, waiting to see what kind of reactions occur from the unconscious. When the therapist, together with her/his client, tries to understand these messages, she/he is a kind of midwife.

The analytic session is an almost ideal field to gain the data on which scientific depth psychology is based. This is true for several reasons: through the analytical situation, the unconscious is invited to share its messages with the ego. Its messages can be heard and interpreted by the therapist directly, while they are being born and while they are developing, before they can be "corrected" by the ego. The analyst is supposed to understand the language of the unconscious.

Therefore, together with the analysand, he/she can work on the meaning of the message that was inwardly perceived, and, as he/she knows the analysands' outer and inner story of their lives, he/she can observe the interaction between the unconscious and consciousness, as if working under laboratory conditions. Nevertheless, the necessary degree of the analyst's emotional involvement in the process demands quite a bit of critical and self-critical judgement. Due to the training an analyst has to undergo in her/his formation, or due to supervision, she/he should be capable of realising the objectivity scientific work demands.

The science of depth psychology has two aims: first, to explore the language of the unconscious, and second, to explain the structure and function of man's psyche. For these reasons, it is divided into two completely different branches of research: the hermeneutic and the theoretical (see Figure 3). They are fundamentally different because the hermeneutic one applies methods and trains of thought of the humanities, whereas the theoretical branch applies scientific methods. In this regard, too, depth psychology differs from traditional scientific disciplines. According to its nature, it is interdisciplinary: it is a natural science as well as a human science.

Let us look first at the processes on the hermeneutic branch. The aim of hermeneutic research is to find out what the author of a text wants to say. Depending on the kind of text one is working on (text in a very wide sense of this word), one can distinguish between theological, juridical, art historical, archaeological, and other forms of hermeneutics.

The hermeneutic method of depth psychology is concerned with the meaning of the creations of the unconscious. Such creations can be found, on the one hand, in fantasies, dreams, or visions that have been collected by analysts, or, on the other hand, in myths that have been passed on, including the Christian myth summarised in the Credo. Other creations of the unconscious can be found in legends, fairy tales, alchemical scriptures, psychological and theological mysticism, for example.

According to depth psychology, all creations of the unconscious are messages that the self—the leading authority located in the area of the unconscious—sends to the ego through inner perception. The messages are sent in a metaphorical language that helps to illustrate mainly psychic processes, phenomena that are not concrete and can hardly be imagined.

As this metaphorical language is no longer immediately under-stood by the ego on today's level of the evolution of man's conscious-ness, the creations of the unconscious must be interpreted and translated into our modern language, which contains more and more terms, notions, and definitions. The hermeneutic work of scientific depth psychology primarily concentrates on the interpretation of archetypal images and of motifs of activities, that is, the archaic ele-ments that were mentioned above. The results of this research were later applied by analysts to their daily work with clients. Thus, we can say the analyst's work is mainly hermeneutic.

The exploration of the meaning of metaphorical language fol-lows a method similar to that of comparative linguistic studies. One result was that the messages of the self could be divided into four groups: (1) messages that correct one's way of life; (2) messages that give an aim to one's life; (3) messages that give a sense of mean-ing and purpose; (4) messages that explain things or provide illumi-nation.

A condition of applying the hermeneutic method in depth psychology is knowledge of the specific structure of the metaphorical language of the unconscious. This method of observing processes is similar to that of linguistics. Although the self mainly uses images that are known to us from everyday experience, such as a house or flat as symbols representing our consciousness, or a lake or the sea as sym-bols representing our unconscious, one must be aware of the fact that the self can become creative in its own right and create its own images, symbols, and metaphors. Thus, it creates figures such as demons to illustrate disintegrating tendencies of our psyche, tenden-cies which urge the ego to ignore the limits of human knowledge as well as the limits of things the ego wants to do: these figures consist of elements of images that are familiar to us but which do not actually exist in this world around us.

If we look at paintings of the devil, the Christian demon, we will see a human body, cloven hooves or claws, horns, and the tail of a cow or a dragon. With all these elements that can be perceived through our senses in this world, the self creates its own language, and composes a figure that cannot be sensually perceived anywhere in our world.

In analogy to this process, the self illustrates psychic laws and developments. So, the emergence of a new attitude towards things in our everyday life is often illustrated by a baby naturally begotten, whereas if something emerges that is extraordinary and maybe important for a whole epoch, the self uses the paradoxical symbol of a supernatural procreation: the mythologem that a god impregnates a human virgin and that she bears a divine child. On the other hand, the mythologem of the suffering, the death, and the resurrection of a god illustrates the psychic law that a fundamentally new attitude can only be integrated if one has suffered from the old outdated attitude and if one has abandoned it completely because of that experience.

The aim of the theoretical branch of scientific depth psychology is to evaluate the observations won from research, and to develop models that explain the structure and function of the ordinary, as well as the disturbed, psyche. As depth psychology arose from the efforts to understand and to treat neuroses, thoughts about their pathology, pathogenesis, and treatment played an important role from the beginning. Hence, a great number of theories of neuroses and therapeutic methods developed. This has led to various schools, each of which concentrates on a special segment of the whole spectrum of psychic disturbances.

Thoughts about the structure and function of an ordinary psyche were of secondary importance. They occurred in the background and did not become as well known as those of neuroses and therapeutic measures. However, this new model of the ordinary psyche had a deep impact on our view of man and of our world.

It is this model we will concentrate on now.

This model had already been developed in the first two decades of depth psychology, that is, between 1900 and 1920. It is still valid today, and it has been reconfirmed by many positivistic disciplines in the meantime. If we look back at the genesis of this model, we can distinguish two phases: the first is connected with Freud and the second with Jung (see Figures 4 and 5).

Freud still conceived the unconscious as something that developed in the course of a person's individual life as a consequence of suppressing and forgetting. That meant the unconscious was believed to have a disturbing effect on a person's consciousness. Jung belonged to the second generation of explorers of this new science. Although he basically confirmed Freud's model, he differentiated and enlarged it considerably. Their models are related to each other just as—*mutatis mutandis*—Newton's theory of gravitation is related to Einstein's theory of relativity.

By 1920, Jung had completely developed his model. Unfortunately, he never systematically presented it with all its various aspects. The reason was that, after 1920, he concentrated almost exclusively on the exploration of the language of the unconscious. This is understandable, since his great achievement was decoding the ciphers of this language. (After the discovery of the self, this was Jung's second most important pioneering achievement.)

Another reason for his concentration on the hermeneutic aspect was the strong interest he had had for a long time in the world of images, symbols, and metaphors created by the unconscious. Ideas about his model of the psyche, which were constantly in mind while he was carrying out hermeneutic research, were somehow subconsciously disseminated throughout his hermeneutic writings. That is why they were spread all over his work.

Another reason for neglecting the theoretical aspect so thoroughly might be that Jung, characteristically, did not express himself very precisely, even if that sometimes confused his audience. This was regrettable, I think, because Jung's theoretical insights were the real reason that he was able to overcome the archaic worldview, at least theoretically.

In the 1970s, when the relevance of Jung's insights became obvious during the interdisciplinary efforts to develop a view of man that was adequate for modern thinking and that was empirically scientifically founded, his widespread theoretical statements were gathered together to be understood in their specific contexts for the first time. After that, all the elements were arranged as a whole, just as, in a puzzle, the many individual pieces eventually make up a complete picture. Only then could the importance of this brilliantly simple and coherent model be recognised.

Although his model was more than fifty years old by that time, and the growth of knowledge in the sciences of living beings had been extraordinarily great, it was still valid. It even became obvious that new insights of positivistic sciences confirmed and supported Jung's model.

In this short book, space does not permit me to go into detail, but I have presented Jung's achievements and their history in my previous books, for example in: *Archetypen – Natur und Kulturwissenschaften bestätigen C. G. Jung* (Archetypes – Natural Sciences and Human Studies confirm C. G. Jung) (Obrist, 1990).

Now let us have a look at Figure 4. Naturally, this is just a scheme of our psyche. Something that is abstract has no representation at all. However, as we cannot imagine anything invisible except in spatial categories, we must illustrate it in graphic or similar models.

One can choose different ways of presentation. I have finally decided to represent the psychic "field" by a circle and the centres that are capable of "data processing" by a dot. In my model, I could neither illustrate psychic dynamism nor the evolutionary depth of the centres—especially that of the self—nor the character of the objectivity of the unconscious. Therefore, I shall describe it verbally.

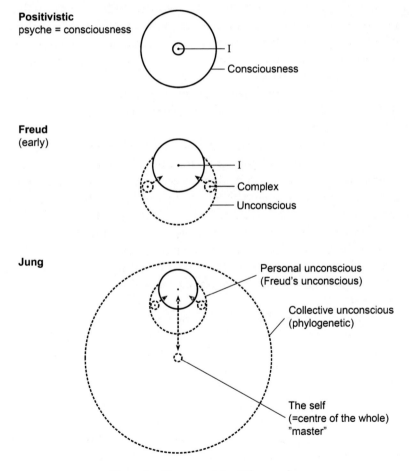

Figure 4.   Three models of the psyche.

To my mind, Jung's most important discovery, which was the basis of all the further discoveries, was the discovery that the unconscious was phylogenetically acquired. Jung called it the "collective unconscious", because our modern biological terminology was unavailable to him at the time. The expression "collective" led to many misunderstandings. Many people believed that Jung meant to say that there was something like ether that engulfed the whole earth and in which all individuals participated. Once a student asked Jung how he understood the collective unconscious, and he answered by explaining that "collectiveness" could be illustrated when one looked at one's liver, which was of the same kind in all people, and each person had one from birth. In other words, with the expression "collective", he wanted to say that the unconscious was acquired phylogenetically. Besides, Jung wanted to distinguish the collective unconscious from Freud's ontogenetic unconscious, which Jung called the "personal" unconscious.

The idea of ether might have emerged from the fact that there is direct communication between consciousness and the unconscious—not indirectly through our five senses.

It is that type of information that seems to be relevant when we talk about the reading of thoughts, fortune telling, or about group dynamics or communication during mass events. Jung was not thinking of all these phenomena when he talked about the "collective unconscious", although he studied such phenomena, too.

Nevertheless, among biologists, Jung's thesis of the phylogenetic nature of the unconscious met strong rejection. That is not surprising in view of the fact that the conception of living beings, and even of nature altogether, was still extremely mechanistic and materialistic in those days.

Today, it is common for well-informed biologists to talk about the phylogenetic nature of the human unconscious. Since the early days of ethology, it has been known that animals have extraordinarily highly developed structures that enable them to recognise something and behave in a certain way, but it is also known that animals are not aware of those capacities. It could be said that each kind of animal has got its own typical unconscious. One has to keep in mind, though, that the term "unconscious" is a term used and developed by depth psychology, because depth psychology branched off from the psychology of consciousness, as mentioned above. Biologists prefer to use the word "pre-conscious" because their way of thinking follows the evolutionary axis upwards. To them, therefore, animals are living beings that have not yet acquired consciousness. This is the kind of linguistic problem that has to be solved before you can work inter-disciplinarily.

Each species of animal has an unconscious cognitive system as well as an anatomic physiological one. Both systems are phylogeneti-cally acquired. The unconscious cognitive system comprises all the "innate" knowledge and all the know-how that an animal needs to live and to survive in a world that is largely inimical. This know-how has steadily increased during the course of evolution through the con-frontation with our continuously changing environment. For this reason, Konrad Lorenz called biological evolution a process in which knowledge is gained. The know-how that is typical of the vertebrates has reached its highest level in what we call the human unconscious. Out of this fertile ground, human consciousness has grown—that is, the capacity to distinguish between the ego and the non-ego, or between subject and object.

Jung's second great discovery within his theory was that of the self: the leading centre of our whole psyche, including our conscious-ness and its centre, the ego. This concept, too, was misunderstood, and rejected by the biologists for a long time for the same reasons as their initial rejection of the phylogenetic unconscious.

Here, I would like to comment briefly on the misunderstandings: although Jung founded the theory of the self, as well as the theory of phylogenesis, empirically, based on his observations of psychic phenomena, it was viewed mystically by many of his pupils. The main reason was that most of his students had not studied natural sciences, but, rather, humanities or theology. So, for example, one of Jung's first students, Marie-Louise von Franz, who studied ancient humanities, sometimes talked about a cosmic, and sometimes even about a divine, self. His disciples accepted this misunderstanding and passed it on in many publications.

First of all, this was done by theologians. The misinterpretation of Jung's conception of the self was again passed on after the 1968 revolt in the USA by the protagonists of the New Age Movement: Capra, Maslow, Ken Wilber, and others. They were inclined to this view because they were familiar with their Indian gurus' gnostic ideas, including their mythical idea of the "core" of the human psyche.

Maybe Jung himself enhanced this misunderstanding, through his strong liking for gnosticism. It was there that he hoped to find confirmation for his discovery of the "self". In his memoirs, Jung mentions that after the "guild"—the acknowledged elite of psychologists—had rejected his model of the unconscious, he asked himself whether "he had fallen out of mankind". In that moment, he felt a great relief when he found the notion of "Atman" in Indian scriptures, and in the "Inana Yoga", an almost pure development of the Gnostic type of religion, the "pleroma" is called "Brahman" and the "residue of divine substance" in man is called "Atman". It was believed that consciousness had no direct access to "Atman", but that he would inspire consciousness. So, Jung saw in Atman an analogue to his self.

From today's perspective, it is obvious that we must assume a completely different genesis for these two ideas. According to the Gnostic view, Atman poured down from heaven and then slipped into a human body. The self as conceived by Jung, however, came from "beneath", that is, it was the final product of the "rising" evolution of living beings. Maybe Jung was not even aware of this difference, or maybe he did not consider it necessary to mention it. Anyway, it would be very improbable and hard to believe that he was not aware of the difference between a mythical view and an empirically based theory. However, because Jung often repeated his view that gnosticism had understood the essence of the psyche better than Christianity had done, he somehow encouraged the misunderstandings.

To obtain a more clear and exact understanding of Jung's conception of the Self, it might help to look at Figure 5, which shows the flow of information that takes place within our psyche as well as the one between the psyche and our external world. The model is based on the cybernetic principle. Let us take the position of the ego in Figure 5. There we can see how two different flows of information run towards the ego: sensory perception and inner perception.

Sensory perception that, according to its definition, pours through the senses into the psyche, mainly reaches the unconscious region. Only a small part reaches the ego. Since Kant, we know that our sensory perception does not exactly convey the external world to us, not the way it really is "in itself". Kant introduced the distinction between "world and worldview", a distinction on which today's often hypertrophing constructivism is based. One could argue against this kind of constructivism by referring to Konrad Lorenz, who says, in his

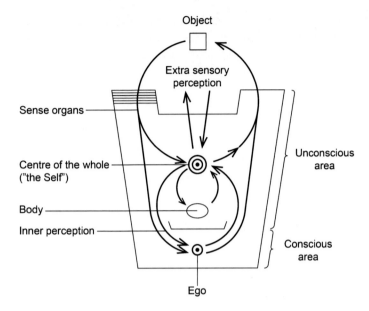

Figure 5.   The flow of information within the psyche and between the psyche and the external world.

evolutionary epistemology, that animals that did not perceive their environment adequately were eliminated by selection.

Inner perception flows from the self to the ego. Different from sensory perception, it conveys analysed information to the ego. It is the self that integrates the various incoming streams of information. These are (1) the manifold qualities (optical, acoustic, etc.) of sensory perception that reaches the self from the outside; (2) perception from one's own body; (3) extrasensory perception (not through the well-known sensory organs); (4) feedback from the ego. In the sense of cybernetic information processing, all these flows of information are finally compared with the "innate" programmed targets.

As a result of these processes of integration, the self sends effective impulses into the external world or into the body, or through the channel of inner perception into consciousness or to the ego. Depending on the condition of consciousness (being awake or asleep, or being in an even more extraordinary condition), these messages reach the ego through daydreams, dreams, or visions. They are encoded in a metaphorical language. As I said before, it is the task of the hermeneutic branch of depth psychology to decipher this language.

Before we continue, I would like to describe how scientific research proved the mystifying conceptions of the self to be pure speculation. It was the Swiss neurologist Gino Gschwend who did so—unintentionally—when he explored the overall integration system, which covers wide areas of the cerebral cortex. To enable a better understanding of his achievement, I shall present a summary of his studies in a wider context. It might also serve as an example to support my earlier statement that Jung's conception has been confirmed in various ways by positivistic sciences.

Let us presume the model of depth psychology implies the notion of "self-regulation". By conceiving the unconscious–conscious psyche as a self-regulatory system with a main and a subordinate centre (the self and the ego), Jung anticipated the systemic view of nature by some decades: it is that view of nature which, since the 1950s, has replaced the purely analytical, and especially the mechanistic, view in biological sciences. One insight, essentially contributing to the systemic view, is that nature itself has applied the principle of the feedback regulatory circuit for three billion years. In particular, molecular cell biology has drawn attention to this fact. It proves that the countless programme-directed processes in a cell can maintain the process of living only because these processes are regulated, controlled, and interlinked with each other in a wide network.

After the step to multi-cellular organisms, the principle of regulatory circuits, interlinked with each other, continued on higher levels of complexity: on the level of tissue, organs, and organ systems as well as on the level of an organism. In the course of biological evolution, it is nerve tissue that has specialised in regulating. In the context of the hierarchy of the inner organisms, slowly a hierarchy of neural regulatory centres emerged. Each of them is autonomous to a certain degree, but only if it concedes some of its rights to higher ranks.

Finally, at the top of the hierarchy, a centre emerged that controls the whole organism by taking into account the somatic, as well as the psychic, aspects. Regulatory circuits presuppose information flow and data processing. Because this process occurs unconsciously on all levels of an organism, one has to enlarge the common notion of the unconscious. Generally, we can say that reality, which we call the unconscious, reaches far down into the cells.

With more and more effective methods, neurobiology has, step by step, discovered how the nervous system functions on the different levels. Today, a point has been reached where neurobiological results confirm those of depth psychology. The point where the two sciences meet is the leading regulatory centre mentioned above. Neurobiology calls it an integration system that has a command centre, the integrator, which has a complete overview of, and controls, all unconsciously operating autonomic integration centres. Depth psychology calls this integrator the self. In this way, the two strands of research met. Both had initiated the discovery of the unconscious in the nineteenth century, although coming from different directions. First, the breakthrough occurred in the "psychic" branch, and then, in the 1970s, in neurobiology, too.

Further exploration had already been carried out in biology by 1906, when the Englishman Charles Scott Sherington, who discovered the function of the neuron (Nobel prize 1932), postulated a central system of total integration, situated in the cerebrum. Nevertheless, it took decades of neurobiological research before detailed studies could prove this postulation to be correct. First of all, the scientists had to become aware of the high degree of complexity of neuronal interaction on this top level.

Finally, in the 1970s, the breakthrough occurred. Following his teacher, the Swiss Nobel Prize winner Rudolf Hess, who had discovered the location of the instinct centres in the diencephalon, and the location of the sleeping centre in the thalamus, the neurologist Gino Gschwend started to explore the whole integration system, which he called the "integrator" for short. This largest network of neurons of the human cerebrum, which consists of eighteen smaller systems, proved to be the leading regulatory centre that receives information from everywhere—from the outside and from within the organism. Because of this input and its phylogenetically acquired knowledge, the global system continuously designs patterns of behaviour that are suitable for each situation and it sends these patterns into the musculature (also into that of the organ of speech). At the same time, it provides the energy needed through the vegetative nervous system. In addition, it sends impulses to the "I", which emerged from it. In the language of depth psychology, these impulses are called "creations of the unconscious".

All vertebrates have an integrator. According to the terminology of depth psychology, one can say each organism of this species has a self. In principle, we can even say each protozoon has a self, albeit a very simple one. Even if it does not have a nervous system, it is able to recognise its food, to draw energy from it, to transform this energy into an energy sufficient for its organism, and to carry out programmed nourishing and consuming processes of metabolism as well as complicated processes of partition, etc. The fact that the co-ordination of all processes in a protozoon is integrated or regulated by one control integrator allows us to speak of a self. The processes that evolutionary biological cognitive science focuses on are essentially those of the growth of complexity in such "selves".

Gschwend imagines the emergence of consciousness—and, consequently, that of the ego—during the ontogenesis of a human being in such a way that, during the course of the first year of life, certain neurons of the global system spontaneously become active in a special way. As soon as that happens, the global system starts to integrate itself; it starts to reflect things. In the interaction between ego and self on which depth psychology focuses, the topic is the interaction between the very small area of the integrator that is capable of self-reflection, or self-integration, and the very wide area of the integrator, which realises the unconscious overall integration.

Through knowledge about the way that the overall integration system functions, there is also more clarity about the problem of free will that is still discussed today: the ego does not only reflect on things but can also act deliberately. In the positivistic view of man, the ego was considered the only force of will, but now, from the point of view of depth psychology as well as of neurobiology, it proves to be a guided leader. Like all regulatory centres of the inner organism outside the unconsciously acting integrator, the ego has only relative autonomy. The lower centres—from the cell upwards—can be called relatively autonomous because they relinquish some of their competences to a higher central authority, whereas the "I", the free will, can be called relatively autonomous because it hands some competences down to the overall integration system, or the self, which is "under" the ego from the evolutionary point of view.

The course of evolution has produced this result. While neuronal hierarchy grew upwards from the ground, the ego originated as a subordinate centre in the integrator: it was dispatched by the integrator into a freedom that was only relative. All these observations help to understand the fact that in the creations of the unconscious, the ego receives corrective and purposeful impulses.

Knowledge about the integrator also explains more clearly the evolutionary step from the animal primate to man. From the neurobiological point of view, the fulguration of consciousness occurred through the circumstance that the integrator, with only a few spontaneously active neurons, became capable of self-integration. According to this point of view, the further evolution of consciousness was based on the fact that more and more spontaneously active neurons had continued, step by step, to foster the self-integration of the global system. In this process, at each step, new, secondary cognitive abilities fulgurated, such as the ability to develop syntax, to conceive a terminology, or to do mathematics.

The process of individuation

There is a phylogenesis of consciousness and there is also an ontogenesis of consciousness: a development of the ego in the course of an individual life. The result of a human child's development from an unconscious being to an ego that takes place in the course of the second year of its lifetime can be compared to a bud. Like a bud, the ego is meant to grow, according to its phylogenetic programme, into a well-shaped ripe fruit. The phases the ego goes through during the so-called process of individuation were discovered by Jung. To be more precise, he discovered the succeeding phases of psychic individuation, and out of these phases he mainly explored those of the second half of the human lifetime.

Individuation does not only occur with people. It takes place with all multi-cellular organisms. With the evolutionary step to multi-cellular organisms, individual death came into the world and, between birth and death, the realisation of one's phylogenetic programme through the phases of youth, adulthood, and old age. Individuation does not happen independently of one's environment, but in facing one's world.

Individuation in unconscious living beings takes place naturally, so to speak, whereas with man the process of individuation is often difficult. At least, this is true for the mental, intellectual, and psychic process. Jung compared individuation to the sun, which seemingly rises in the morning and sets in the evening. Concerning the eclipse, mental–intellectual individuation differs from the psychical one. The intellectual one principally follows the physiological development of the body. In the first part of one's life, intellectual and physiological individuation strive for power, energy, vitality, and resistance. In the middle years of one's life, the development reaches a maximum, after which it declines again with advancing age.

Psychic individuation, however, is different. First, it is something that cannot be defined quantitatively, but which is rather a qualitative development that can be compared to the ripening process of a fruit. Second, the phylogenetic programme arranges for this process not to reach its maximum in the middle years of a person's life, but, rather, to consider these years as a turning point, after which the psychic process takes a different direction and steadily continues advancing until the end of a person's life.

In the first half of one's life, it is essential for psychic individuation to go out into the world and to develop a strong ego that can face the various challenges of the world. After the middle years of a person's life, the phylogenetic programme demands that he should free himself from too close an entanglement with the world but not lose his acquired abilities, and, in addition, to develop those qualities which were neglected or repressed during the phase of going out into the world.

When accompanying processes of individuation, one first of all pays attention to the impulses coming out of the unconscious. In this process, Jung recognised the following development: at first, the ego is urged to dissolve its identification with the "persona"; that is, to feel identical with the "face" one shows to the world and which is, to a great extent, conditioned by the job and the social position one has. Then we have to become aware of our "shadow" and integrate it; that means we have to integrate all the—mostly negative—attitudes which were suppressed in the unconscious during our phase of going out into the world, as I said before. When this tiring and often painful task has been successfully accomplished, the analysand is urged to differentiate his relationship to himself and to the world, which means acquiring a relation to his ego that expresses adequate self-confidence, and a relation to other people that expresses something of the Christian value of charity to one's neighbour, for example, and, finally, it means improving the relation to one's self. The last task has proved to be the most difficult one because of the dominating role of the ego based on the positivistic understanding of oneself. However, only the true realisation of the relation to the self enables the individual to differentiate the two kinds of relations. This step would also be a remedy for the illnesses of our Western world.

In the context of his observations of the functions of a relationship, Jung designed his model of "anima" and "animus", a model that I believe is still very helpful in understanding our psyche. However, as this model has been severely criticised recently, especially by feminists, I shall not discuss it any further here. I shall, rather, phrase the problem of differentiation slightly differently from the way Jungians usually do.

In the context of the relation between ego and self, Jung made his famous statement that the religious question would sooner or later arise in the course of the process of individuation. A great number of theologians thoughtlessly abused this statement and maintained that Jung had meant the return to the lap of religion. Jung, however, did not talk of religion when he made this statement, but of religiousness. He meant that religiousness as a human attitude belonged to the species-specific programme of human individuation. I shall return to this aspect later.

Before doing so, I want to mention that Jung conceived the programme of individuation as species-specific because he had noticed that processes of individuation followed the same pattern again and again, in spite of individual variation. Besides, the impulses coming from the unconscious confirmed his impression that something regulated the whole system from there. All this reaffirmed Jung's concept of the self.

Depth psychology: an existential science

An adequate relation to the self has been reached if an individual is ready to pay attention to the self's messages and to take them into consideration when making a decision, even if they contradict the person's conscious intentions. Experience shows that later on it is usually found to have been right to follow the self.

This attentive attitude that makes a person act in a way that is in accordance with the self has been called "religiousness" in our occidental tradition. The word is derived from the Latin word *religere* (pay attention to, follow the laws). The Romans used this word to describe an attitude that makes a person ready to listen and pay attention to the will of the numinous invisible powers when a decision has to be made. As the Romans still held the archaic worldview, they assumed that the numinous beings lived outside this world, in a world beyond. After the second step of the mutation of consciousness, however, it became known that these powers "are deep inside our souls"; they are the phenomenon that Jung calls the self. With Jung's internalisation of the traditional conception of a supernatural world and its supernatural beings, an essential step in the course of the change of consciousness was taken.

Although I think that the word "religiousness" adequately characterises the human attitude that I described above, in what follows I am going to use the word "spirituality" instead, simply because for many people the word "religiousness" has negative connotations. It is often associated with religion, church, maybe even with affected piety. One reason for the difficulty in understanding that "religiousness without a religion" would correspond to today's level of consciousness is the fact that it presupposes sufficient knowledge about the mutation of consciousness, and that is rarely the case. For that reason, I prefer talking about "spirituality", although I do not consider this term really adequate nowadays because of the many diffuse and abstruse esoteric ideas of "spirituality". These ideas do not characterise the attitude that I call religious.

Nevertheless, the term "spirituality" has already found its place in religious studies in the context of "schools of spirituality", for example. Through these schools, we approach a topic that will have to be discussed while we are discussing depth psychology. Before starting the discussion, a conceptual distinction has to be introduced between an objectifying and an existential attitude. An objectifying attitude tries to find out how the things of this world are structured and how they function. Everything I have written about depth psychology, so far, presupposes this attitude. The realisation of the way of individuation, the finding of the "right" way, demands an attitude that is known as existential. While the objectifying attitude concentrates on "truth", the existential one concentrates on "rightness" or "correctness". Both attitudes are needed to fully realise our human traits, to be fully human beings. Both attitudes relate to each other in a complementary way. In each situation, one can choose only one attitude; one has to decide which one to choose.

The peculiarity of each of the two attitudes can be understood best when one looks at the socio-cultural achievements that have emerged from professional efforts to achieve these two attitudes: sciences and the schools of spirituality. Under the dominance of ideological positivism and through the rapid expansion of sciences, most schools of spirituality have disappeared, however, although they had been highly developed in the days of the archaic worldview when modern sciences did not exist. (There might have been one little exception when scholasticism developed.)

Theologians did their work from an objectifying point of view by reflecting on the existence of the supernatural world and supernatural beings as well as on this world, here and now. In the schools of spirituality, however, one strove to please "God" or the "gods". In Christianity, this happened in the religious orders of monks and nuns; in Islam this was looked for in the communities of Sufis, and in Hinduism in the schools of Yoga. Even Buddhism was just a school of spirituality at the beginning, and became a religion only later. A Chinese school of spirituality was Daoism.

In Europe in the Middle Ages, universities and religious orders still existed as equally high-ranking institutions and were complementary to each other. On the one hand, the majority of nuns and monks hardly cared about erudition, though, on the other hand, almost all teachers of theology were members of religious orders and had gone through a training based on the existential attitude. It often happened that great scholars were masters of spirituality, too. I wonder how the situation in theological faculties at modern universities is today. I have not explored it, but I doubt that spirituality still plays the important role it once did.

The fundamental difference between sciences and schools of spirituality becomes most clear when their way of learning is considered. The aim of sciences is to acquire a great amount of matter-of-fact knowledge, and, once it has been gained, it can be put into the store of tradition. In principle, it cannot be lost again. Each generation of scientists can go on doing research on the foundations laid by previous generations. In this way, man's knowledge about nature and culture continually increases. Progress and confidence in progress are the integrating elements of sciences.

Progress of that kind does not exist in the schools of spirituality, because their aim is not the increase of matter-of-fact knowledge, but, rather, the qualitative change of an individual's consciousness. That there have been spiritual reformers who phrased the spiritual aim in different words, or suggested new forms of living, or of exercises due to a changed consciousness as a result of the differentiation of material as well as intellectual culture, could be called progress. However, this phenomenon of new spiritual masters does not change the inexorable fact that in each generation each individual, in his striving for spiritual maturity, has to start at the very beginning: that is, each person has to go through the same kind of experiences and has to make the same kind of mistakes that his antecedents did.

In spiritual training, learning does not mean accumulating a great amount of data, but being ready and open to deepen one's individual awareness. This can happen through surprising and illuminating experiences, through disintegrating tendencies in an individual's soul, through suppressed feelings and wishes, but also through latent capacities slumbering in a person or through questions about the meaning of life.

In this case the "teacher" is essentially a person who has achieved a certain mastery of spiritual life through experience: he or she is a person who has acquired a high degree of consciousness, who knows "God's ways" and how to deal with the attacks and temptations of the "evil spirit". The spiritual master mainly teaches his or her pupil by living in an exemplary way the kind of life that he or she expects the pupil to live.

The essential point of growing awareness through spiritual training, however, is the deep insight that reaching this aim does not depend on the ego's intentional will, but mainly on "grace", the grace of a power that is superior to the ego, but also cares deeply for the ego. The core of spiritual training means to adopt and internalise the attitude that I described above as "religious". Whether this attitude establishes itself in the way I pointed out still depends on the self. Processes of individuation like those in the schools of spirituality are about nothing but this existential attitude. For this reason, depth psychology differs from all positivistic sciences and can be called an existential one.

The impact on the archaic and positivistic worldview

Now we can turn to the question: "How far has the dilemma between knowledge and faith been transcended by the discovery of the unconscious?"

Relativisation

As I said before, both traditional kinds of understanding oneself and one's world were relativised. For a long time, both sides had thought of themselves as being absolute. That means neither of the two groups of scholars and scientists "came out unscathed". However, relativisation had quite a different impact on the positivistic materialistic view on the one hand and on the archaic view on the other hand. While the positivistic view was enlarged, the archaic one was completely turned upside down. This revolutionary process meant that the dimension of reality that had commonly been thought of as "supernatural" turned out to be as natural as anything else.

The dogma of ideological positivism was that everything that is not perceivable through the human senses does not really exist. I have already mentioned that the narrowness of this dogma was negated, at least theoretically, when Freud proved the existence of inner perception. This was the argument needed to prove that information about objective reality, which cannot be perceived through our senses, nevertheless succeeds in getting into our consciousness. Here, we can talk about objective reality because the unconscious, by definition, is a non-ego. This conception of an "objective psychic reality" is a basic one of depth psychology.

Although positivists usually have great difficulty in accepting this fact, it must be said that they should see that the blowing up of their dogma actually does not mean a loss, but, rather, the opposite; it is a great advantage, because, through this new point of view, a completely new dimension of reality became accessible to research, a dimension that had been cut off through the narrow conception of empirical reality. The new and wider conception did not have consequences for the traditional natural sciences such as physics or chemistry because their scientists could go on sticking to methodical positivism. However, the impact on human studies of the widening of the conception of empirical methods and empirical reality was immense. For this group of sciences, depth psychology has even become a basal discipline, in the same way that physics was for the other natural sciences.

The archaic worldview was at least theoretically relativised when Jung proved that the spontaneous impression received during a vision deceives the individual: the visionary does not see a concrete event that really takes place outside in the external world, he only believes that he does so. The images and pictures the visionary "sees" are illustrations of psychic realities that are sent to the individual's ego from the unconscious by the self. The impact of this proof was so strong because religious science traced back the contents of faith of all religions to reports of visionaries, given that enough historical sources were accessible. The role of visionaries is commonly known with regard to the Jewish and Islamic religious tradition, but is less known that even the central Christian mythologem—the belief in Christ's resurrection—goes back to visions, to the so-called Easter visions, especially that of St Peter.

When these results of religious science were first discussed, for many people the interpretation of a vision by depth psychology was hardly known, and even today many people do not accept that the images in a vision should be just creations of the unconscious and not phenomena of a supernatural world. As most people nowadays know hardly anything about visions, perhaps I should briefly inform the reader about the phenomenon of a vision.

The vision

Visions are not to be mistaken for hallucinations, the key symptom of schizophrenia. They are as common as dreams, but they do not occur as often as dreams; mostly, they appear only when a decisive step in psychic development has to be taken. Consequently, the experience of a vision is extraordinarily intense. A single vision can turn a person's life in a completely new direction. From experience with analysands, we know that visions mostly occur when the unconscious has insisted on a change for quite a while without any reaction from the analysand. He just does not pay attention to his dreams, or heed the message from the unconscious.

Today, people are usually reluctant to talk about their visions because they are afraid of being declared insane. The reason for this fear is that psychiatry is still positivistic. In the analysing praxis, fortunately, one meets visionaries now and again and has a chance to explore their experiences. In the past thirty years, I have met thirteen people who have had visions. One reason might be that it must have become known that I am very interested in visions and that I have intensively studied reports about visions and their contexts for years.

The vision is a central subject of depth psychology, but its point of view is mainly hermeneutic: it tries to understand the sense of the images and symbols that are seen in a vision. However, my area of interest is the vision as a process, the "physiology" of the vision.

First, we have to keep in mind that visions force themselves on a person. He cannot suppress them. The visionary passes from the state of being awake into the so-called extraordinary state of consciousness, a state that is often called a state of reverie, ecstasy, or trance. In this state, the person cannot be talked to and is insensitive to pain. Often the person even goes into a coma, and, when he awakens, he surprisingly maintains that he has been awake all the time, even more alert than usual. Concerning our question, it is decisive that the visionary says that everything he saw took place outside himself, and that it was even more real than anything he had ever experienced.

Phenomenologically, two types of visions can be distinguished. In most cases, the visionary event takes place in the limited area of one's field of vision, so that our environment can be perceived, even if only at the edge of it. This type was called "apparition", and it meant, from the archaic point of view, that the phenomena experienced here were believed to be supernatural, other-worldly beings that had revealed themselves to a human being. If the visionary is in a state of coma, however, as he seems to be to the observer, he often has the impression of being carried away, either to a different place on the earth or into the supernatural world. The experience of this type of vision is called "reverie", or "being carried off". At take-off and just before he returns, the visionary can look down and see his body, which he left behind.

To illustrate the message that the self wants to convey to the ego in a vision, it chooses images that are familiar to the visionary through his/her socialisation. The metaphorical language the self uses is essentially the same as the one it uses in dreams, but it is more intensive. The different individual background of each person is the reason why a Christian visionary, for example, sees Christ, the Blessed Virgin, the angels, and the devil, as well as canonised saints, whereas a North American Indian from the tribe of the Oglala-Sioux reports that he met the "holy horses" in the colours and with the insignia of the "four holy directions" above the clouds, and that he also found a tipi in which the six great deities of his religion were sitting, who gave him a bow and a holy pipe on which an eagle's feather was hanging in approval of the message they gave him to carry out his mission.

The reason why there are so many different "heavenly worlds" and such a variety of other-worldly populations beyond our world is simply the large number of images of the many human cultures from which the self can choose.

Jung's discovery that visions are creations of the unconscious led to two different effects: in the context of the mutation of consciousness, the first and most far-reaching effect was the overcoming of religion, because if one concluded that the phenomena one had believed to be supernatural beings were just creations of the unconscious, or illustrations of psychic powers, religion as a socio-cultural community with archaic rites would lose its meaning. Then only religiousness, the existential religious attitude would be discussed. It would mean that the theologians would lose their epistemological basis—the archaic conception of revelation. Indeed, the foundation of the Catholic clerical church has started to crumble: that is, the belief that the rites of an ordination give an ordained person supernatural powers from the moment of the ordination until the end of his life, so that he is able to perform sacramental rites effectively and, thus, to open the way to heaven for lay people.

One has to admit that Jung was never completely able to draw these conclusions from his discoveries because, in the deeper layers of his soul, he stuck to the archaic worldview. In his old age, he did so even more strongly than when he was younger. That shows that, even for Jung, the following old experience was true: great explorers have very seldom recognised the full impact their discoveries might have on the future.

Projection

The second far-reaching result of Jung's insights about visions is that they enable us to understand how the archaic worldview emerged and developed. When looking for an answer, we have to pay attention to the fact that the visionary is deeply convinced that he sees an event that takes place in the external world, although the images flow from the inside, from our unconscious to the ego, the centre of our consciousness. In depth psychology, this process is called "projec-tion". In technical language, one says the things seen in visions and great dreams are perceived in projection and, because of that, conceived as something concrete, as something that is capable of exist-ing independently. From this experience, a worldview was conceived, or this experience was integrated into an existing worldview.

The term "projection" is misleading, however. It was introduced by Freud in analogy to those technical instruments which are used to project slides or films on a screen. In this technical projection, the pro-jected picture is really outside, on the screen. In a vision, it is differ-ent; the visionary merely has the impression that the things he sees are outside. In fact, the vision is an inner psychic process that produces an illusion that can be compared to an optical illusion.

In Figure 6, I have tried to illustrate the spontaneous impression a person has in a vision. However, it must not be understood as a phys-iology of projection.

The state of consciousness that occurs in a vision is really extraor-dinary, and this is so not only because of its difference from the common states of being awake or being asleep. "Great" projections presuppose this exceptional state of consciousness. How this inner

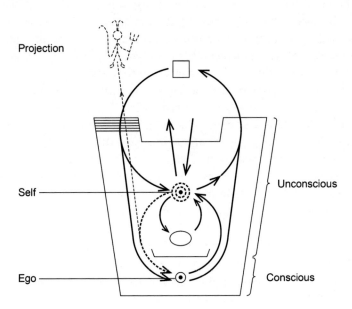

Figure 6. Projection (cf. Figure 5).

psychic process works physiologically, nobody yet knows. However, that lack of knowledge is not really pertinent, and neither does it question Jung's model. It is like the situation of a neurophysiologist who cannot explain the fact that we perceive brightness despite its being dark in the cerebral visual centre.

The process of projection was discovered by Freud, but only in its everyday, or weak, form. Thus, he recognised that persons with an unconscious power complex, for example, were often convinced that they were free of ambition for power, and, in addition, they even thought that there were power-hungry people everywhere around them. Freud said that these people projected their own repressed ambition for power on other people. However, it must be conceded that the repressed emotions were usually only projected on such persons who had some propensity that would provide a hook on which the projection could be hung.

"Great" projection was discovered by Jung in the context of the exploration of visions. Nevertheless, it has to be considered that the phenomena perceived in an "everyday" projection and in a "great" projection come from different layers of consciousness. The projections of one's own negative qualities which I mentioned above come from the Freudian unconscious, which Jung calls the "personal unconscious". It is the layer that is directly under the threshold to consciousness, and in which repressed feelings loom and develop into intense emotional complexes which can have an irritating impact on the ego, and which can be "deferred" by analytical therapy.

In the "great" projections, however, we are faced with matters from deep layers, matters that were called "archaic residues" by Freud, but that were later called the archetypal contents of the collective unconscious by Jung. That means we talk about figures and events that are composed by the self out of impressions that seem to be perceived through the senses, but actually do not exist in the external world around us. The impression is fertile material that conveys meaning to people. In addition, it enhances the evolution of consciousness.

Nowadays, knowledge about the "great" projection enables us to understand how once the archaic worldview, with its supernatural and usually invisible worlds and beings, developed. On the relatively low level of consciousness in former times, the "things" visionaries talked about in reports about their visions, dreams, and even daydreams, were concretely interpreted and believed to be physically true. In those days, visionaries were respected as authorities concerning supernatural matters, as prophets of divine messages. The histories of various religions mention them again and again.

Through Jung's discovery that the spontaneous impression in a vision deceives us, the development of the archaic worldview could be understood and even overcome, at least theoretically. The "supernatural" world was reduced to the level of nature, and in this process it was "deconcretised". Hence, a categorically new view of the world has become possible, a worldview that allows the evolution of consciousness to advance. In everyday language, one could say that through Jung's discovery of the "great" projection, archaic man's supernatural world was incorporated into man's psyche. At the same time the two archaic patterns of behaviour, magic and rite, were overcome, whereas another pattern, prayer, survived and is still a meaningful pattern of behaviour. I shall return to that topic later.

Not only did the view of supernatural worlds and beings have to be deconcretised, but also the concrete conception of objective mental reality had to be changed. This had developed—as I said before— because the other-worldly beings had been increasingly imagined as immaterial. Thus, metaphysical concretism developed, because no one had yet been able to recognise the deceptive nature of spontaneous impressions received in visions.

Now, 500 years after the days when a concrete conception of the objective mind threatened to hinder any further advancement of the top level of the evolution of consciousness, this old conception has been overcome by the discovery of projection.

However, the whole supernatural world was not incorporated into the psyche. A large part of objective mental reality remained outside. This part was also derived from the supernatural world, but was not integrated into the psyche but, rather, into nature, into living as well as not-living nature, including our human body. We will see how this model can be understood by remembering how the dilemma between faith and knowledge was transcended by natural scientific research. Before discussing this question, though, we shall have a closer look at the various notions, ideas, and images of God.

CHAPTER FOUR

The impact on our conception of God

R eligious sciences distinguish between gods as creators and as deities close to man. On a primitive level, all great deities embodied both divine qualities. The slow but steady process of the moving apart of these two conceptions can be observed historically in the Ancient Egyptian Empire in the so-called Shabaka inscription of the theological scriptures of Memphis. In that early phase of the Egyptian Empire—after 3000 BC—"the pushing up of heaven" was realised to such an extent that the creator of the world—Ptati the Very Great—was considered to be transcendent. That meant that the theologians were faced with the problem of explaining to the people how this god, who was so far away, transcending everything that could be comprehended by man, could hear people's prayers and smell the smoke of their offerings.

The problem was solved by the paradox of the essentially equal divine son, whose essence is the same as the one of his father, and who is, at the same time, close to the people. Then the Egyptians "recognised" God's son in the sun as a solar being. About 2000 years later, the father–son theologem was integrated into the Christian idea of God as Trinity.

Since Christian belief claims monotheism to be true, the two persons—Father and Son—are melted into one person through the Holy Spirit, who is also part of their unity. For our reflections, however, we have to distinguish between the "two persons" for the time being.

Religious sciences say that these two different ideas of God belong to the two different categories of myths: the myth of the creator God belongs to the explaining type of myth and the myth of the God who is close to man belongs to the religious type. The reason for these two different types of myth is that each type has a different genesis.

The figure of the creator of the world has resulted from the reflection on the question "How did the world come into existence?" It is a figure that has an integrating function in all the innumerable myths of creation that ethnographers have collected from all over the world. Until the modern age, the cognitive means for empirically and scientifically founded studies to answer this question did not exist, and so illusions and fantasies filled this vacuum of knowledge, as is true of all myths that try to explain nature in metaphorical language.

The figure of a god that is close to man, however, has not been the result of abstract reflection on the beginning of the world, but is the result of personal experience. It is the inner experience of a power that is superior to the ego, a power that can illuminate, but also punish people for wrong behaviour. The experience of this inner power is the constitutive element of religious myths. The fact that the inwardly perceived power was interpreted concretely as an other-worldly being, was due to the opacity of the process of projection in those days. It was not until the beginning of the twentieth century that the model of projection was discovered and developed, as described in the preceding chapter. It should be expressly stated here that the notion of "God" is no longer needed in the new worldview, and neither are the dualistic pairs of terms: theism–atheism, transcendence–immanence, nature–the supernatural. These terms became obsolete, like the notion of "God", after the dualistic dilemma had been transcended. In order to understand this, however, we have to look at the new conception of objective mental reality. Only through this new conception has a new view of man and our world become possible. It is a world free of the notion of "God".

A new conception of objective mental
reality leads to a new worldview

To convey the meaning of this essential notion of mental reality as clearly as possible, I would like to repeat that objective mental reality means a kind of mental reality that had been there before consciousness or, in other words, subjective mental reality, came into existence. In analogy, that was seen similarly in the archaic worldview in which the gods in the various myths had always existed before man came into existence.

The breakthrough to the new view of objective mental reality became possible through natural sciences, as mentioned before. Shortly after 1900, the so-called energy paradigm was formulated, which manifested a worldview that philosophers called materialistic. After Einstein had proved the equivalence of mass and energy, it was believed that it would be possible to reduce all processes of nature—including the epiphenomenon of the human mind—to energetic processes that physics could explore and analyse.

Later in the course of the twentieth century, this ontological reductionism, together with scientifically founded materialism, was overcome by discovering more and more phenomena in nature that could not be explained through the quantifying physical notion of energy. That meant there were phenomena that were not quantifiable.

The insight that not everything is quantifiable emerged when evidence was given of the structure of an atom. Wolfgang Pauli, the great pioneer of quantum physics, pointed out that an atom can only be understood if it is considered to be an entity: that means being more than just the sum of tiny parts. It represents something that cannot be grasped through the physical notion "energy". In the following decades, other large numbers of notions, such as "entity", were introduced into natural sciences: complexity, self-regulation, system, autopoesis, spontaneity, self-organisation of matter, information, cognition, communication, behaviour, etc. All these empirically founded notions could not be understood or explained through the physical notion of energy. Hence, a new categorical term for all the phenomena had to be found.

The notion "mind", a term used in our occidental tradition as the counterpart of the notion "matter", seemed to offer itself as an adequate categorical term for all these aspects of nature newly accepted by the sciences.

Since the 1970s, more and more top natural scientists have supported the opinion that ideological materialism has been overcome and one should introduce the notion of "mind" or "mental reality" again. Of course, the newly introduced term had to be compatible with modern knowledge of nature.

In the discussions of our study groups about this topic, I pointed out that, when trying to comprehend objective reality, we would have to take into consideration the kind of functioning of our consciousness. That meant that we would have to divide those newly discovered aspects of nature into pairs of terms. At the same time, we would have to use the notion "complementary", a term introduced by Niels Bohr, a fact that was, unfortunately, hardly noticed for a long time by scientists outside the world of physics. Then I emphasised that in our time we should use Bohr's complementary approach when talking about the two main dualistic pairs of terms: "matter–mind" and "body–soul". This would mean that it was no longer necessary to distinguish between matter and mind, but only between the material aspect and the mind aspect of a holistic spatio-temporal reality. With this train of thought, the "aim" of the mutation of consciousness, the transcending of the concretism of our idea of mind, or mental reality, has almost been reached.

First, however, it had to be clarified how these two aspects could be distinguished by taking into consideration all the knowledge then available about nature. Then one day, Erwin Nickel, a mineralogist at the university of Fribourg, Switzerland, incidentally mentioned, "Today, matter is usually defined as structured energy." That remark was the key I had been looking for. That definition contains two statements: (a) matter consists of energy; (b) energy is structured. One would have to ask two questions about each spatio-temporal phenomenon including everything from an atom up to a human being: (1) *What* is structured here? (2) *How* is this "what" structured? If one asks "what?" one gets the answer "energy". That means the answer points at the material aspect. If one asks "how?" the answer is: "it is a kind of structure or order that cannot be comprehended or defined by the traditional physical notion, 'energy'". We called the new notion of being structured the "mind", or "mental aspect" of nature.

When observing how being structured has become more and more complex in the course of evolution, one becomes aware of the necessity of an increasingly multi-faceted conception of objective mental reality: that is, the mental aspect of nature. To comprehend this aspect as differentially as possible, Einstein's distinction between "compact" energy (energy condensed into atoms) and "free" energy (in physics traditionally called "powers") has to be considered. In each of the two states, energy has been structured in an increasingly complex way in the course of evolution: in the "compact" state through spatial arrangement into morphological structures, and in the "free" state through temporal arrangement and directing into processes. In either state of energy, in the morphological structures as well as in the processes, one can distinguish between the material and the mind aspect of nature.

Evolution had so far been explained materialistically, but with Einstein's approach to energy, one phenomenon in evolution could be better understood: the dynamism in evolution which has led to increasingly complex arrangements but which could not be explained with the traditional physical notion of energy. While it is the natural quality of energy to adhere to the law of gravitation and to destroy forms and increase the entropy of the universe, it is just the opposite with evolution. Here, we can become aware of a dynamism that points in the opposite direction: it does not destroy forms, but creates more and more complex forms. As this dynamism cannot be explained using the traditional notion of energy in physics, this form of energy has to be attributed to the mind aspect. A very special aspect of objective mental reality manifests itself in this free energy: creativity in the true meaning of this notion. When looking at this natural creativity from today's level of consciousness, we can understand why, from an archaic point of view in earlier times, the conception of a supernatural creator of the world emerged.

The results of this creativity are also the fulgurations that occur at each evolutionary step towards a more complex system and bring about completely new qualities and capabilities. If we want to know which fulguration was most important for people's search for a modern, adequate conception of religiousness, we will find that it is the evolutionary step to life, the step to living creatures. It was the emergence of something called "inwardness" by Adolf Portmann: the capability for cognition, for innate knowledge, for analysing and evaluating information, etc.

When observing the continuously progressing growth of complexity of the unconscious cognitive system, we can recognise how that phenomenon which we call the human unconscious has developed: the term human unconsciousness describes the most complex realisation of that aspect of objective mental reality which one calls inwardness. When observing biological evolution, this inwardness must also be taken into consideration along with the above mentioned morphological and functional aspect (cf. my more detailed description in the book *Die Natur – Quelle von Ethik und Sinn* (Nature – A Source of Ethics and Meaning, Obrist, 1999). So, the notion "unconscious" is perfectly suited to our modern conception of nature, although, in the very beginning of depth psychology, it seemed to be outside the field of natural sciences. If we choose this new perspective, then, in front of our eyes, the new conception of man, including its pair of terms "ego–self", and the new conception of the world, including the material and mental aspects, will fit together to create a new understanding of ourselves and our world. The view is categorically different from both the archaic and the positivistic one.

All this means that the human self is not seen as a solitary monade, as some critics repeatedly claim. First, from the point of view of biological evolution, it is the most complex development of a structure that is supposed to be the structure of even the simplest beings. That means, if we look at the line of genomes, we find the self in a sequence of all lower selves.

Second, we have to take into consideration that, at least at the level of the human beings, a direct communication between unconscious and unconscious, between self and self, takes place. The flow of information that is being referred to here is the phenomenon that is dealt with in parapsychology. If this phenomenon is subsumed under the notion of co-evolution of living reality, one becomes aware of the fact that the self of each human being is embedded in a powerful stream that can be called the creative facet of objective mental reality.

Now it might be easier for the reader to understand what I meant to say when I stated that in the new worldview, the notion of God would no longer appear. Indeed, the mutation of our consciousness can be compared to those great steps of biological evolution at which a new plan of a structure was developed, such as the step from amphibians to reptiles, or that from reptiles to mammals.

While new morphological and physiological plans of the organisms developed at these steps of biological evolution, at the step of the mutation of consciousness a new cognitive plan developed. That meant people gained a fundamentally new understanding of themselves and their world. It is fundamentally new because, by means of turning the apperception of inwardly perceived information through 180°, former structures of thinking are changed and our thinking is directed to a new track, just as a train would be after the switches have been worked.

While "man" and "God" was the constitutive pair of terms of the archaic worldview, the constitutive pair of terms of the new worldview is "subjective" and "objective" mental reality. One has to remember, though, that mental reality means that aspect of nature that is complementary to the material aspect. The expression "subjective mental reality" (consciousness, or ego) corresponds to that which was called "man" in the archaic worldview. The expression "objective mental reality" corresponds to the traditional notion of God, and implies both former types of ideas of God.

If one understands objective mental reality as the creative potential which caused all evolution, it corresponds to the archaic creator God. If one looks, however, at the result of the evolution of inwardness to human consciousness, to the human ego that can inwardly perceive the self directly, then this notion corresponds to the archaic God as man. (Christian theology speaks of the Son of the Almighty Father.)

The conception of man changes

Now we can realise the change in the conception of man, which I have mentioned several times before (cf. Figure 7). With the archaic worldview, people in Christian countries felt as if they were "walking under the eyes of God". In every respect, people felt dependent on the "divine grace" granted to them. They also knew that their minds were limited and needed inspiration through the divine spirit. Besides, they believed that after death they would have to account to God for their deeds.

The positivistic–materialistic self-concept, however, supposes that the only mental reality in the world is human reason, the phenomenon we call consciousness today. Reason is believed to be such a great light in us that it can enable us to enlighten the remotest corner of reality, and to recognise those deeds that are good and those that are bad. In

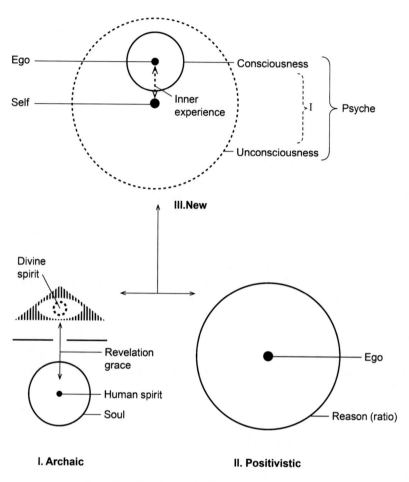

Figure 7. The change in the conception of man.

the twentieth century, Europe, especially painfully, experienced what subjectivist ethics resulting from this positivistic self-concept led to.

Since the discovery of the self and of projection and the resulting internationalisation of that which archaic people called the "God as man", one has recognised that the source of norms of ethics is within the human psyche. In this way, the ego is again connected with the self and feeds back the ego. That means, with this second step of the mutation of consciousness, ethics are again founded in the objective psychic dimension.

Thus, it finally became possible to adapt ethics to the new level of consciousness that had been reached in the meantime. It was a process that had been necessary for a long time. It will be described later.

A contradictory process loosens firmly established positions

Here, just one thing should be kept in mind: if one really understands what has happened through the mutation of consciousness, one holds something like a compass in one's hands. This instrument can help you to find the way through this chaos of opinions that is typical of a phase of transition. Evolutionary steps are irreversible, but it has to be kept in mind that they do not occur everywhere at the same time. As mentioned earlier, they occur at the evolutionary top level of a population and only very slowly diffuse into wider and deeper layers. One reason for resistance against change is widespread neophobia.

Even today, this diffusion has barely happened, but at least it seems that the ground has been prepared quite well for this new worldview. For a moment, let us look backwards to see what has happened so far. At the beginning of the twentieth century, archaically minded people and positivists faced each other with firmly fixed contrary positions concerning the dilemma between reason and faith. The churches formed the archaic bloc, while sciences formed the opposing bloc. Despite the fact that there was quite a large number of Christian scientists, many of them always reverted to the archaic view of the world when going to church. Thus, these people could be regarded as members of the archaic side, especially when they tried, and still try, to distinguish themselves through philosophical essays or through discussions at academic congresses as strict defenders of the archaic point of view.

Even during the first half of the twentieth century, neither the archaic minded people nor the positivists realised that this dilemma de facto had been overcome. In the course of the second half of the twentieth century, the narrow-mindedness on both sides was loosened and became wider, at least subconsciously. This process occurred in both factions, but led each side in the opposite direction, a phenomenon that can also be observed in an individual's process of change. In depth psychology, this process is called enantiodromia (from Greek: *enantios*—contrary; *dromos*—course/run).

Enantiodromia within the positivistic bloc

Enantiodromia took place in the positivistic bloc through the transition from the mechanistic–deterministic conception of nature to the systemic one. This development started with the modification of the conception of causality. The first step was taken with the emergence of the quantum theory, which replaced determinism and its monocausal foundation of the conception of nature with the statistical one. And when cybernetics started to develop after the Second World War, the linear conception of the cause–effect process had to be replaced by a circular conception: the model of a circuit of self-control says that the effective outgoing impulses are continuously corrected and, in this way, the conditions of the impulses perceived from the outside, too. This has led to the insight that, in nature, all phenomena are linked with one another through circuits of self-control.

The conception of causality was once again modified through the chaos theory, particularly the discovery of the fact that the laws of nature are not linear. It became increasingly obvious that, with most processes of nature, it is not possible to take into consideration the totality of all marginal conditions. That means, in traditional language, that you cannot grasp all causes of a phenomenon. In any case, this development showed clearly that "determination" had been overcome and notions such as "range of variation, bifurcation, accident", etc. had found their legitimate place in the description of nature. The other component of the deterministic–mechanistic conception of nature—the mechanistic view of living reality—was overcome by the emergence of the notion "system". This development had already started with the so-called debate on holism in the context of quantum theory: it started with the insight that atoms can only be understood as entities that are more than just the sum of their parts.

When the age of biology replaced that of microphysics, the notion "system" as a key term for the description of nature prevailed: the idea of a dynamic totality that controls itself and that is able to transform itself while maintaining its totality. This transformation, too, takes place through self-regulation. Evolutionary higher systems proved to be capable of learning, of changing their immanently programmed targets because of experiences. All these new aspects were not in accordance with the image of nature as mechanical clockwork, and so the mechanical conception of nature was replaced by the systemic. As the function of systems could only be fully comprehended if the final aspect was also considered as complementary to the causal aspect, the notion of "finality", which had been rejected and scorned for centuries, achieved a legitimate place in the language of natural sciences.

In spite of this change in the conception of nature, all exploration of nature—even that of living beings—still followed the energy paradigm, whose essence is materialistic. This paradigm was discovered almost at the same time as the unconscious.

By the end of the nineteenth century, natural sciences had worked out two generic terms in a laborious process. These terms were thought to be suitable to cover all perceivable phenomena. These terms were "energy" and "mass". Energy was abstracted from the quantity of forces (mechanical, electrical, magnetic, thermic); mass, however, was abstracted from the behaviour of material things. Their behaviour had something in common: the resistance against being pushed and against acceleration. It was thought that mass and energy stood next to each other like two domes, without being linked at all.

Then Einstein showed that the quality we call mass is the result of a process in which energy is immensely condensed and can durably exist, enclosed in baryons and leptons. That leads to the conclusion that matter consists of energy. Einstein also postulated that mass can be transformed into free energy and that free energy can be transformed into mass. He even described the factor of the conversion: it is a factor beyond the normal human capacity of comprehension, for the units of measurement have been concluded from the explorations of mass and energy: the factor is the speed of light squared (e^2).

Since that time, the term "energy" has been used as a new, enlarged generic term: it was a term that, like a roof, comprised all spatio-temporal dimensions of reality that could be realised and analysed through scientific methods. After that, one had only to distinguish between free energy and energy condensed as elementary particles. This view of reality is what I call the energy paradigm. After having found this paradigm, many scientists were convinced that they would be able to reduce all processes of nature—the process of life included—to the notion of energy. This point of view can be called "ontological reductionism".

Soon, however, an increasing number of top scientists became critical of this materialistic view of nature, and more and more alert people became aware of the fact that, subliminally, a categorical change of the concept of ourselves and of our world had taken place.

In order to recognise what this change was about, one had to overcome the kind of naïve realism that had led to "absolute" reductionism: it was based on the belief that we were able to fully recognise the world as it really is, to see the things themselves. First of all, people had to understand the anthropic revolutionary thought that Kant initiated more than 200 years ago. It meant that people had to become aware of the fact that they had to distinguish between the world in itself and the world perceived by man. They had to find out and fully realise to what extent they could recognise the world, and how efficient, or, conversely, how limited their innate cognitive system was.

These questions could no longer be clarified just by philosophical speculation because, in the meantime, empirical research on cognition had successfully developed, and, in the course of this development, depth psychology, with all its implications, emerged.

Under these circumstances, the breakthrough, described above, took place in the 1970s. It was the result of interdisciplinary efforts to develop a new view of human beings and their world. The discoveries made then have not yet been widely disseminated in our society. Nevertheless, through the enantiodromic process in the archaic bloc, at least the ground has been prepared for the new view.

Enantiodromia in the archaic bloc

Enantiodromia took place in the materialistic bloc because of discoveries their scientists had made. That meant the valid energy paradigm was no longer compatible with the new results. So, here, enantiodromia took place in the context of a process of growth, whereas enantiodromia in the archaic bloc was the result of an "infection". Theology had not only stagnated for a long time but it had also "inhaled" a deadly "virus": critical historical studies.

Theologians seemed to believe that in this way they could make their discipline look like modern sciences. As archaic people, they were not aware of the fact that the message of the incarnation of God's son was a myth, a myth that projected the idea of God's incarnation, his freely sacrificed life to redeem mankind, his resurrection, his ascension etc., on the historical person of Jesus. Thus, quite a few theologians mistook the gospel for a historical report and did not realise that it was a historicised myth. For some time, the theologians had no idea what a strong impact the introduction of critical historical studies into theology would have on Christian "truth".

As far as the history of the church and of the popes, the laws of the church, and theology were concerned, the confrontation with this new, critical, historical point of view did not seem to be dangerous or threatening, but when theologians started to explore the genesis of the Bible, of the Old and especially the New Testament by applying the historical–critical method, enantiodromia began. It became obvious that the "Holy Scriptures", considered thus far as God's word, consisted of scriptures written by human beings, that the evangelists had melded Jesus' message and his religious belief with the message about the historical Jesus and his might that had developed within a few decades of his death into a historic report. In this way, the projection of the myth on the historical Jesus, which had already happened, was established.

When historical research on the compilation of texts tried to find out what each evangelist had slipped into his text from his own conviction, or from the community he lived in, for example, one recognised that even Jesus' life story had been composed. So far it had been considered to be a true historic report. So Mark, for example, created little scenes fitting to the supposedly authentic words of Jesus that had been handed down. Out of these scenes and some other separate stories about Jesus that had been handed down, he created a "life of Jesus", which later served Matthew and Luke as a model. Besides that, historical research on compilation made it obvious that the evangelists—John especially liked doing so—often placed elements of the Christian myth into Jesus' mouth, and later on these statements were believed to be authentic words of God. Especially disillusioning was the insight that the rite of the Eucharist, which is a central Christian rite, was not established by Jesus himself.

Historical–critical research showed that the holy words spoken during the consecration of bread and wine, through which, according to Catholic teaching, an ordained priest can effect transubstantiation, that is, the true presence of Christ, must have come into existence in the time after Easter, after Jesus' resurrection. These words were introduced to legitimise the ritualised acts that had developed in the early Christian communities, which means that these words were integrated into the rite of the Eucharist in which the Christian myth had started to be dramatised.

The exploration of the early days of Christianity helped to show how the Christian myth had developed. It showed that the belief in the resurrection of Christ was based on visions, especially on St Peter's vision, and it also showed that the idea that Jesus was the Messiah spread in Jerusalem's early Christian community only after Christ's death, when most Christians there still thought of the Messiah as a human being. In addition, these studies revealed that the idea of the Messiah (Greek: *christos*) as a divine being entered the Christian myth only after missionary work had been done among the Jews of the diaspora. It also became obvious that the idea of equating "Christos", who had become a divine being by that time, and the "Logos"— the Greek notion of the "Son of God" whose essence is identical with that of the transcendent God—did not occur earlier than in the bosom of the "pagan-Christian" communities.

Besides, comparative religious studies showed that the "message" about Jesus consists only of mythologems—motifs taken from myths—that also existed in other cultures: for example, (a) the mythologem of the "Son" whose essence is identical with that of his divine Father; (b) the mythologem of incarnation through being born of a virgin; (c) the mythologems of the inconspicuous birth and the pilgrimage on earth of a divine being who offers a new law and a new revelation to the people; (d) the mythologems of suffering, death, and resurrection, linked with (e) the mythologem of a God's redeeming sacrifice of life, etc.

The inner decay of the firmly established archaic bloc caused by historical–critical research did not become manifest for quite a while because, in the 1930s, "triumphalism" emerged in Catholic theology, and Protestant theology was strongly influenced by dialectic theology which implied an archaic tendency. When looking back today, one gets the impression that these two theological schools were a kind of last rising up of a critically ill organism.

Then, in the second part of the twentieth century, a massive—inner and outer—emigration from the churches started.

In spite of this development, the representatives of the Christian churches—not only of the hierarchically structured Catholic church— have stuck to their traditional doctrines and the way of proclaiming the "word of God". It seems as if, in the eyes of the church leaders, the comparatively few Christians in Europe are regarded as a *quantité négliable* and as if they think they can rely on the large number of Christianised populations outside of Europe whose consciousness was—and still is—deeply embodied to quite a large extent in the archaic worldview, which implies loyalty, keeping old traditions, and looking for the security that rites, norms, and authoritarian structures can offer.

At the same time, there is obviously also a strong need for religiousness in Europe, in spite of the exodus from the churches. This need for religiousness, or spirituality, leads to various abstruse ways of realisation because this need wants to be fulfilled, even though the result of the mutation is not yet known. For this reason, we shall look for conceptions and exercises of spirituality that might be suited to modern consciousness, to people living today.

CHAPTER FIVE

New spirituality and ethics

"Spirituality" is a very vague term. If I use it here, I intend to describe the attitude that I called "religiousness" in the chapter about individuation. In Christian tradition, one usually used the term "faith" (Latin: *fides*) instead of religiousness, but this term must not be used uncritically.

It must be considered that theology has distinguished between "faith in something/someone" and "certainty of faith": in technical terms, between: *fides quae creditur* and *fides qua creditor*—faith in something, some truth that is believed in on the one hand, and the faith through which one believes, the act of believing, on the other hand. Uncritical ideas of supernatural beings and naïve trust in Christian doctrines of salvation, for example, have been overcome by the mutation of consciousness. It has been replaced by empirically founded knowledge about the forces of the human psyche and their impact on the ego.

The importance of the certainty of faith, the act of believing, however, has not been questioned by this new consciousness. Just the opposite, it has been recognised as absolutely necessary for psychic maturation. So, in processes of individuation, for example, one can again and again observe how this process suddenly gets started and turns to becoming more than just theorising ideas: exactly the moment when the analysand feels the certainty that he can trust the hints or the advice coming from the unconscious, and that one should follow the instructions of the self, even if these instructions seem to be diametrically opposed to one's conscious intentions.

Furthermore, we do not call an attitude "religious" before this absolute trust (*fides qua creditur*) has established itself. Before this attitude has been achieved, it is just a striving for religiousness. This striving is essential, though, because it is the condition that certainty needs in order to manifest itself. However, pure will alone cannot bring about this certainty: it establishes itself. When accompanying processes of individuation, one can again and again observe that, all of a sudden, this certainty occurs.

This certainty cannot be forced to appear. It just appears because the self wants it to do so. This process depends on the "discretion" of the self, symbolically speaking. It is the process that is considered to be the effect of "divine grace" from the archaic point of view. Depth psychology has not found a more appropriate expression to characterise this process. However, there is one difference: grace is not considered to be something that is poured down from heaven, but is thought to be an inner psychic process.

Besides that, it must be mentioned that there are two different tendencies originating from the self, integrating and disintegrating ones, tendencies which strive for entireness and those which urge the ego to transgress the limits of thinking as well as the limits of acting. As far as thinking is concerned, this urge is positive, because it allows the evolution of consciousness to go ahead. As far as acting is concerned, the result—unless there is optimisation—can be something we traditionally call morally evil: evil thoughts, words, or deeds.

This ambivalence of the self has also become manifest in traditional conceptions of gods. One can easily understand such a reaction in man if one takes into consideration that archaic people perceived the illustrations of the self as "god as man" in their projections. So, in early religions, the ambivalence of the self took shape in concrete images of gods that were good as well as evil, such as Shiva in Hinduism, for example. In Christianity, the two tendencies have clearly been separated: on the one side the good ones are attributed to Jesus Christ, who is always the good one, and on the other side, the bad tendencies are attributed to the devil, who is always "the tempter" and evil.

Because of knowing about the conflict between these two forces to which man has to face up, Christian spirituality thought it indispensable for every Christian to become experienced in "discerning spirits", to learn the ability to distinguish the different "movements of the soul", to recognise which is "the voice of God" and which is "the voice of the devil". Theologians usually maintained that they "knew" that the devil would finally give up when faced with Christ, but it was necessary that the Christian believer truly strove for "the discipleship" of Christ. The difficulty in "discerning spirits" can also be observed in the processes of individuation. That means one has to be able to translate metaphorical language into everyday scientific language in order to understand its message. This language has to be adequate for modern consciousness and for our modern view of man. This means, in our case of the process of individuation, that we have to learn to distinguish between the aims of our ego and the impulses and advice given by the self.

Certainty of faith nowadays

Let us talk again about man's striving for religiousness. We have to realise that any kind of existential attitude requires considerable effort, but this is something that a person who is shaped by positivism has to learn again. This fact is not taken into due consideration when the evolution of consciousness is purely intellectually realised, as, for example, by the philosophy of Enlightenment, which maintains that man is good by nature, and if a person was only rationally and clearly enough told what is right, this person would be able to act in the right way. Analytical experience, however, has endorsed the experience that archaic people never doubted: that the temptation to act evilly is intrinsic to human nature, and that constant efforts are needed to resist this temptation.

Modern society quite strongly longs for more and more knowledge and it is unquestionable that everybody has to strive for it. Thus, we spend quite a bit our lifespan on education. In most cases, we need and want only factual knowledge, knowledge we obtain through empirical research. To be successful, it seems, we need an objectivising point of view in contrast to an existential point of view, which we need for spiritual education. When comparing the time we spend on the acquisition of factual knowledge with the time we spend on spiritual education nowadays, we will notice how miserably small the latter part is. Also, the governments in most countries financially support cultural and educational life, but hardly promote or support spiritual training.

How to use the know-how of the schools of spirituality

Until the mutation of consciousness, true faith meant the faith in something or somebody. For this reason, religiousness had always been linked with religion. Now, after the supernatural world of religions has been relinquished and the religions have been deprived of their foundations, today's religiousness, which is adequate for an up-to-date level of consciousness, is religiousness without religion. It is much more difficult to achieve a religious attitude without religion than if one was embedded in a religion. Religions are communities of rites. By enacting the rites again and again, the believer absorbs the "eternal truths" of his religion revealed by God. By doing so, he automatically assimilates the right behaviour towards God to his consciousness.

However, there are rites as well as magic practices that lost their foundation after the supernatural world was relinquished. It is different, though, with prayer, which is no longer seen from the archaic point of view: praying is no longer talking to a god or another supernatural being outside of our world, but it is talking to the self. Knowing that the ego is linked with the self, we can better understand the effectiveness of praying in the context of the new worldview.

Believers who practised "religiousness with religion" lived in the world of their religion and profited from the rich tradition of a careful cultivation of spiritual life: they benefited from the know-how acquired through the various strivings for religiousness. As I mentioned before, this know-how had been acquired professionally in the "schools of spirituality". The various practices that had been tested repeatedly were very helpful for the believers.

This know-how was mediated in a master–disciple relationship. The function a master had in the schools of spirituality would today be attributed to the analyst who has been trained through experience in studies and exercises of depth psychology. The analyst should realise this function primarily as a "psychagogist" rather than as a therapist. Today, though, most analysts work as therapists because, in our modern society, there is a great need for therapists, much greater than in earlier societies, because quite a large number of people suffer from psychic deficiencies.

A therapy is only a first step in reaching the real aim that has become obvious through the discovery of our species-specific unconsciousness: this aim can be made conscious through psychagogic methods, through which a person can be accompanied on his or her way of individuation. Knowledge about these methods should not be limited to analysts only. Their know-how should be disseminated and made known to everybody who is involved in educational work. The typical modern educator, who is still shaped by the positivistic worldview, should become a psychagogist. This would mean catching up with the development that has taken place through the mutation of consciousness.

It seems to me to be extraordinarily important to recognise that psychagogics should find out and continue the core of the tradition that was kept and taught in the schools of spirituality based on the archaic worldview. Unfortunately, this wisdom of spirituality has become lost to a great extent, due to the general "evaporation" of Christianity.

However, this know-how about spirituality could be discovered and worked on again, as it has been preserved in a great number of scriptures—in Christian scriptures as well as in those of the other great religions. In Christian tradition, we can read about this know-how in the scriptures of the Anchorites, in the rules of their orders, and in the comments on them, in the letters of guides of the soul, in reports about mystic experience, in symbolic descriptions of the "way of the soul", in autobiographies of great religious people, as well as in scholarly books on spiritual life.

We have to keep in mind, though, that the know-how in those days was still phrased, written down, and passed on from the archaic point of view. Formulated in that traditional context, it is hardly accessible to people nowadays. If we want to profit from that old wisdom for our present way of individuation, we have to distinguish the knowledge about spiritual experience from its mythical background and translate it into a language that is suitable for today's post-mutation level of consciousness. The decoding of the metaphorical language of the unconscious has made this possible. In the same way as the know-how about spiritual tradition is made transparent and understandable, it is a great enrichment for psychagogic work.

As psychic maturity is the aim of individuation and presupposes a religious attitude, which can only be granted to us by the self, it would be helpful for today's psychagogists to share the knowledge of those traditional "aids" so that their disciples can follow theses pieces of advice in order to enhance the process in which the disciple is granted the "grace" of absolute trust in one's self.

Here are the eight most important pieces of advice.

1. Externally: the creation of a sheltered area by reducing the sensory impressions that shower a person. Internally: by the meditative attitude called the "internalisation of the desert".
2. The various practical methods of immersion (true meditation). I prefer the Eastern ways of meditation to the Western ones, because they support the process of "the head becoming empty" more effectively, and, thus, they make the stream of inner experience flow.
3. Prayer. First of all as an act of saying thanks for enlightening and helping grace, and as an act of pleading for further tokens of grace.
4. Exploration into conscience. That means the process of becoming conscious of one's personal shadow, as it is known in analytical psychology.
5. Regret injustice one has done. The aim was "complete" regret, not because of worldly consequences of misdeeds but because one had offended "God's will".
6. Ascesis (Greek: *askeo*—to practise), originally meaning exercise and training. On the one hand, the decision to give up disordered leanings, tendencies, such as the tendency to be highly sensitive, to be jealous, to crave recognition, to lie, etc. On the other hand, to adopt positive qualities such as moderation, sincerity, indifference, etc.
7. Control of one's conscience at least at the end of each day: the habit of accounting to oneself for the way one has spent the day, to what extent one has succeeded in realising in everyday life what one had decided to achieve through certain "ascetic" efforts.

8.   Reading spiritual scriptures: scriptures that deal with the striving for a religious attitude.

Summing up all these pieces of advice, one could say that all of them encourage us to practise what was called "care of spiritual life". This care was common in everyday life in the Catholic church until Vatican II (1962–1965). Today, this care of spiritual life still exists, but only in a barely noticed corner. Besides, it is hidden behind an archaic language, which is poorly understood by people nowadays. Because of that, it would be an important task for those who have realised the mutation of consciousness to revive this spiritual tradition when accompanying people on their path to individuation. By doing so, one could help to reduce the difficulty of practising and living religiousness without the support of a religion.

Adaptation of ethics

We have seen that with the second step of the mutation of consciousness, the idea of the source of ethical norms has been transferred back into objective reality.

The species-specific frame of human behaviour does not change through the mutation of consciousness. It is just an adaptation of ethics to today's level of consciousness. Again and again ethics were adapted in the course of the evolution of consciousness, principally without its frame being changed.

This can be explained when we listen to ethnographers who stated repeatedly that even in "primitive" societies there were ethically highly developed people. Even if a cannibal thought he would receive the enemy's energy by eating him, this cannot be judged as evil. The cannibal's attitude was just the result of the early archaic worldview. Each differentiation of continuously developing human social life in the course of the evolution of consciousness had its specific impact on the different concepts of ethics.

But how should we adapt ethics to suit today's consciousness? The answer is simple: that will happen because more and more people will strive towards ethically valid decisions as a result of their efforts for individuation. If it should happen that psychagogics became part of common knowledge, the adaptation of ethics would occur by itself.

Consequently, the members of ethical commissions would no longer follow only their rationale or their ideologies, but could, instead, reach a decision by trying to optimise the relationship between the tendencies of the ego and the self.

CHAPTER SIX

At the threshold of a fundamentally new age

O   n the whole, there was a linear development from the Stone
         Age until the end of the Middle Ages. A long row of small
         evolutionary steps led to increasingly differentiated world-
views, but in all of them the myth was seen concretely. Then,
however, there was a radical cut made to this line of development
when the concrete idea of the myth was abandoned, and that led to
the internalisation of the metaphysical world.

The impact of the first step of the mutation of consciousness

First, there was the decline of Christian–Occidental culture. Characteristic elements of this culture were the omnipresent influence of the
Christian churches on private and public life, the Christian–humanistic education system, with its emphasis on ancient culture and occidental classic culture, and the idea of the divine right of the ruler
granted by God that legitimised the governmental structure of the
state and the system of the nobility.

In the twentieth century, the rule of the state by divine right as
well as the religiously justified power of the nobility was replaced by

democracy, which means a state based on the sovereignty of the people. Together with that political development, a colourful civil society emerged outside of the sphere of influence of the churches, less and less shaped by Christianity. In addition, the humanistic concept of education was replaced by the scientific point of view of natural sciences, technology, and economics.

However, we have to keep in mind that positivistic–empirical sciences and technology, as well as democracy, are due to the first step of the mutation of consciousness. A second step has to be taken so that one-sided negative results can be turned into positive "fruit". The negative aspects can be seen clearly today when people talk of a crisis of democracy, or when they are afraid of the danger that science, technology, and economy cannot be controlled or directed any longer, or when more and more people suffer from disorientation concerning the question of what we are and should be, or what we do and should do. This disorientation must be recognised as a negative impact of the first step of the mutation of consciousness and the concept of man resulting from it.

The second step of the mutation of consciousness: catching up with the process of mutation

We have to be aware that the new age can only develop if the second step has also been taken.

In this little book, I have tried to explain what is radically new about this second step. I have tried to focus on the core of the process: the conceptions of the notions "matter–mind", because this is the true, essential achievement of the mutation of consciousness. It is the germ—like the seed of an oak—out of which a strong, all embracing, comprehensive culture can grow, a culture that is equivalent to the occidental culture which has declined. What this culture might look like in detail, we must leave to the future.

At the moment, it seems to me to be most important that the change towards a new concept of man and to a new understanding of oneself must be realised by the majority of people in their everyday lives. Up to now, this change has only taken place theoretically. This would not be so important if people nowadays were not so disorientated in relation to existential questions of their lives, such as: What is correct? What should I do? What is the meaning of my life?

Formerly, the archaic concept of man was orientated towards a divine power, which imparted meaning, security, and a solid aim for life. The outcome of the mutation of consciousness necessarily entailed the loss of traditional security. The concept of man in the Age of Enlightenment, which was centred on the ego, brought about an immense liberation, but it also opened the way for undesirable tendencies: for example, tendencies to egoism and evil that are immanent in man.

Unfortunately, we have to realise that it was this ego-centred concept of man, linked with a subjective concept of ethics, that has led to today's disorientation about existential matters, to the loss of a humanitarian attitude, as well as to an alienation from nature and from ourselves.

Besides that, we have also become aware of the fact that people's power to control the results of science and technology has become weak. The reason is that the feedback through which the ego is linked to the objective psyche has been lost because of the positivistic concept of man developed in the Age of Enlightenment. Finally, we have to realise that today's crisis of democracy is not caused by its legal, juridical, and organisational structure, but by the insufficient maturity of a great number of people who form the democratic states.

To achieve the second step of mutation, it is not sufficient to adopt information about the mutation's course merely intellectually. This is simply the condition for the real transformation of the newly discovered things in our everyday lives. But it means that the pure "homo faber" and "homo economicus" type of man, who is the most powerful and influential type of person in modern society, must really be replaced in concrete everyday life by homo sapiens or, even better, by "homo religious", the latter understood in the secular way I described in the previous chapters from the point of view of depth psychology.

This transformation in our everyday life will be easier for dissatisfied archaic people than for positivists, I believe. The reason is that the essence of this new concept of man, which I have called the religious attitude (the role of the self), is familiar to archaic people through the role of God. Thus, it is very probable that, out of their tradition, the urgently needed equivalent to the notions and ideas they learnt about in their schools of spirituality might develop first. Only through this equivalent—not just through the sciences—is the adaptation of ethics to today's level of consciousness possible. Only in this way can the attitude be achieved that is necessary for the transformation of ethics in our everyday life today.

Prospects for the future

The breakthrough to a new concept of man has happened and evolutionary steps are irreversible. What might happen now is "adaptive radiation" as it is known in bio-evolution: whenever there was an evolutionary breakthrough in one place, various other niches were influenced by the new type of living beings (radiation). Interestingly enough, the new plan of an organism varied with each evolutionary step, adapting to the different surroundings.

As the mutation of European consciousness happened in two steps, there will also be two adaptive radiations. The first has already occurred: the results of empirical research and the positivistic approach—and partly also the positivistic worldview—have spread all over the world. The radiation of the result of the second step of mutation will necessarily follow the natural laws of the evolution of consciousness. This second radiation will be urgently needed, because the first has caused a great deal of misery in Europe as well as in other continents. This misery can only be overcome by catching up with the second step of the mutation of consciousness. This has to be realised all over the world.

The adaptive radiation of the second step presumably will not be achieved as quickly as we would like, after having seen how much suffering has already been caused by the first step. There are two reasons: on the one hand, we see that the breakthrough in Europe has only occurred with people at the top level of consciousness. Before the radiation of the new attitude brought about by the second step can happen, it has to become familiar to, and accepted by, the majority of the people in Europe. On the other hand, the acceptance of this new attitude in other cultures cannot be realised as long as the first step has not been taken, because in this process of the development of consciousness, no step can be left out.

We have to keep in mind that it was only in Europe that an epoch of enlightenment took place and that it was a painful and very long-lasting process that faced the vehement opposition of the churches and the politically powerful rulers who were allies of the churches that had made them rulers by "divine right". Finally, this process had to fight against the opposition of individual neophobic archaic persons.

During the radiation of the first step of the mutation of conscious-ness in continents outside of Europe, the results of European scientific research and the fruit of the inventors' ideas were absorbed as if they were the products of these other continents. No one asked if there would be further consequences. That meant that people neither realised nor accepted the whole impact of positivistic sciences, such as the fact that the positivist point of view eliminated the idea of the "supernatural", or a "supernatural world" out of people's actual worldview.

I would like to state expressly that this is true for the USA, too. The USA has assimilated the political strand of the Age of Enlightenment and they were even the first nation to instigate a legally constituted democracy, but they did not embrace, and were hardly touched by, the philosophical and religious strand of the European Enlightenment. That is not surprising, especially if we remember that all the fathers of the American Constitution were members of funda-mentalist Protestant religious communities. The impact of these reli-gious groups can still be seen when one looks at the intense resistance that exists in many parts of the USA against the theory of evolution and other modern scientific developments.

The tendency towards religious fundamentalism that can be noticed in a very large part of the world—in former times and today—must mainly be understood as an unconscious repulsion of European ideas of the Enlightenment that have spread almost everywhere. It shows that these peoples and tribes have not yet achieved the painful phylogenetic step of evolution. In the end, however, they cannot avoid taking this step because of the psychic laws of the process of death and what arises because of death.

It will require a long period of time before this first step is taken all over the world. Among the occidental religions, at least, slight changes seem to have taken place. In my youth (in the 1930s), for example, when I spent holidays in a Catholic youth camp, Protestants were still called names, such as "sons of the devil", whereas now the Christian ecumenical movement has overcome many barriers among different Christian denominations and has sorted out a great many of the deeply rooted prejudices that are not at all Christian. The fact that the ecumenical movement could not succeed entirely in this is due to the resistance of the hierarchy of the Roman Catholic church, which still maintains that the Catholic church alone possesses the "only true doctrine".

The awareness that religions have lost, or might lose, their strong influence over people has led them to start and to strengthen the inter-religious dialogue among Christians, Jews, and Muslims. While these three religions have been deadly enemies for centuries, now, under pressure, they have found their common roots and call themselves "Abrahamic" religions. However, the mutation of consciousness will only be realised when people have really understood and accepted that the supernatural has been naturalised. That means that neither Jahwe, nor Allah, nor Christ exist as spiritual beings in a supernatural world. Also the Indian, East Asian, and African peoples will have to reach the same kind of insight concerning their gods and spirits.

However, once it has become obvious that the performance of the second step in Europe has not destroyed anything of the existentially important core of the archaic worldview (the trust and confidence in the self), the second step, which permits catching up with evolution, might even be implemented faster outside of Europe than in Europe itself.

All these insights should encourage the Europeans to strive for the implementation of the second step of the mutation. Thus, they could harvest the fruit of their ancestors' work, and a truly new Europe could arise as a Western variation of the culture of the new age.

CHAPTER SEVEN

Autobiographical notes concerning my work

It might very well be that the reader of this short book, which is only a brief summary of my complete work, is interested in the way that my work has developed. The following hints might help to understand my background and my motivation better.

Even if I have often been told that, through my books, I broke something like the sound barrier, I must admit there was very little conscious planning on my side. Rather, I have had the impression that the "self" has guided me clearly so that I could do the work which life seems to have meant me to do.

It seems to me that an important step towards my later development was taken at senior high school, when a teacher of mine, whom I held in high esteem, advised me to enter the religious order of the Jesuits in order to gain access to excellent conditions for a wide education and better training than could be obtained elsewhere. It was felt that would suit my deep and passionate interest in human culture and my social questioning. When I applied to enter the order of the Jesuits, I was asked what my aim in life was, and I answered that I would like to write about the deep-seated reasons for the mental and spiritual crises of the present age. The Provincial, the head of the Jesuits in Switzerland, answered that quite a few people had tried to do so, but in vain. Nevertheless, if I felt this to be my task, the order would offer me the chance to become well trained to tackle it.

Thus, I had the opportunity to study not only philosophy, which was obligatory, but also history, taught by Gustav Schnürer, one of the last exceptionally great historians, I think. I studied the history of the Middle Ages and history of art and German literature as sub-subjects. I started my studies enthusiastically, but when I had finished them, I was so tired of the many contradicting opinions that I was longing for clear, objective facts and statements that could be proved. Besides that, I started to feel no longer at ease with the archaic world-view that was proclaimed by the religious order. That contradictory situation made me decide to leave the Jesuits and to study medicine. For quite a while I forgot my plan to write a book about today's mental crisis, and avidly sucked in scientific knowledge.

After I had successfully got my qualifications as an internist and later as an angiologist, I opened my own surgery and started to lay the foundations for my economic existence. In addition, I went on trying to pursue and satisfy my interest in natural sciences and human studies and so to attain my deeper aim: to satisfy my endless curiosity. I read Jung at first just for reasons of curiosity. It was only after the age of forty that I really became aware of the importance of Jung's work.

While reading his writings, I became at least subconsciously aware that Jung's approach gave me access to the kind of knowledge I had looked for all my life. I also realised that it was not possible to get to know depth psychology just by reading books. Through the description of the process of individuation, I became aware that radical change was necessary, so I decided to give up my flourishing surgery and to apply to the C. G. Jung Institute, Zurich, to enrol on studies to qualify as a Jungian psychoanalyst.

After freeing myself from the obligations of my job as a doctor, I felt that at first it was necessary to study natural sciences to understand and become familiar with the exceptional, almost exponential, progress that had taken place in scientific research since the time when I was a young student. Hence, I studied behaviourism, molecular and cell biology, and evolutionary biology intensively, as well as nuclear physics and cybernetics.

Soon after I entered the Jung Institute, the unconscious called upon me in a dream to make up my mind to do creative work instead of just absorbing things endlessly.

According to the spirit of the house, I understood creative work as the interpreting of symbols. As I considered dogmata to be symbols, I chose a dogma, the dogma of the Assumption of the Virgin Mary, to be precise. This dogma was proclaimed a short time before and was also mentioned in a recent colloquium. During my studies, I had the vague idea that this dogma wanted to say something about a more differentiated view of "material reality". While I was trying to discover how this new view could be achieved, the self offered me the first great insight: I had to find a methodical approach to working on the mind aspect of nature; in other words, on a conception of objective mental reality that is compatible with today's knowledge about nature.

When I looked at the other three new dogmata about the Virgin Mary (Immaculata: free from deadly sin; Mediatrix: mediator of all grace; Co-redemtrix: co-saviour), I came to the conclusion that all the three dogmata were about the "Sophia" figure and that the unconscious postulated an enlargement of the one-sided rationalistic mentality—the extreme "logos view" of those days. When I showed my paper to a Catholic professor of theology (he was a relative of mine), he stated unequivocally, "Dogmata must not be understood symbolically but must be understood literally." He argued that dogmata were based on divine revelation and theologians had special access to it.

In this way, he provided the final incentive for me to start working on the true task of my life, which was to conduct research on the fundamental change in our view of the world and of ourselves. This change took place in the course of the Modern Age, and its deep impact is still felt today. At first, I turned to fundamental theology, whose central subject is revelation. During these studies, I realised more and more that both theology and depth psychology were based on "revealed" things. However, I understood that their ideas of revelation were diametrically opposed to each other. The resulting question was why and how this difference of ideas had developed. Soon, I understood that this was precisely the question that I had asked myself at the age of nineteen, the question which I had forgotten for some time, and which had become more concrete with my more differentiated understanding of the ideas of revelation.

At first, I found myself drawn into the smouldering conflict between depth psychology and theology. I remembered that during my theological studies I had noticed that the theological idea of revelation was based on a cognitive pattern I had become familiar with in my lectures about the psychology of the primitives at the C. G. Jung Institute. From that moment onwards, I started to get an inkling of the fact that in the epistemological foundations of theology and depth psychology, two very different phases of the evolution of consciousness had become manifest. As I was familiar with the evolution of living beings, it was quite obvious to me that evolution had advanced after the emergence of man as the evolution of consciousness. Thus, I had to take a closer look at the evolution of consciousness in order to solve my problem.

The answer to this problem could only be found interdisciplinarily, and it was crucial to find an opportunity, outside the C. G. Jung Institute, for interdisciplinary discussion and exchange. This became possible through the SHG, a new foundation of human studies doing fundamental research. This team consisted of scientists and lecturers working at Swiss universities, and represented natural sciences, human, cultural, social, and political studies, as well as theology, philosophy, and depth psychology. The SHG invited me to participate in their efforts to find out what interdisciplinary work meant and how it should be developed and improved. As I had intensively studied cultural and natural sciences, and depth psychology and theology, too, I was able to profit considerably from these discussions. I obtained a broader and deeper knowledge, which helped a great deal in finding a new point of view from which to answer my question, and it was very important for me to meet people doing research, and teachers of many different university disciplines, among whom were theoretical physicians as well as theologians of ethics, for example. In this atmosphere of constant exchange and disputes, the ideas for my work could emerge and develop.

One fact was especially important, the fact that I was constantly confronted with two prejudices: first, that there had been no "cultural" evolution, as it was known. Second, that depth psychology was not based on an empirically proved theory: the positivists maintained that depth psychology was mysticism and theologians said it was merely philosophy.

That was the incentive that made me look into this matter more carefully and intensively.

During my efforts to prove that depth psychology was empirically founded, I noticed that most of Jung's disciples had not sufficiently explored the theoretical branch of depth psychology. Most of them had worked on the hermeneutic branch, which Jung had founded, too. Jung had done so by decoding the language of the unconscious. In addition, I noticed that Jung never presented his discoveries systematically, although he had been extraordinarily successful in the theoretical field with his revolutionary insights: this is true for his theory of the normal psyche, but not for his theory of neuroses. Neither did he systematically explain or develop the new type of empirical research that had become possible through the discovery of the unconscious. So, I felt that it was part of my task to continue and evaluate his work. It was like working on a roughly cut stone of knowledge.

First, I had to overcome the prejudice that depth psychology was not empirically founded, a prejudice often put forward in the SHG. I had to make the representatives of the other sciences realise the impact of Freud's discovery that dreams were not created by the ego, but were perceived by the ego as complete products of the self. This discovery meant that the positivist notion of empirical reality had to be enlarged by a new dimension, and it meant that depth psychology was mainly founded in this newly discovered dimension of reality, an area of perception that had so far been inaccessible to positivists.

Then I looked through Jung's complete work and collected his theoretical comments, which were scattered everywhere in his many hermeneutic observations. I weeded out all comments that were based only on speculation, and started to compose the remaining statements like a puzzle. All these statements had been empirically proved by observation of the mutual exchange of information between the conscious and the unconscious.

In the meantime, the change from the mechanical view of nature to the systemic one had occurred, and so it became possible to express Jung's discoveries and theses in a language familiar to natural sciences. It was only then that the full impact of Jung's model of the psyche, which he had worked on for years, could be realised and understood by the various scientific disciplines and by the scientists and scholars of all university faculties.

In his model of the psyche, Jung described his discovery that the unconscious is phylogenetic, meaning that its basic pattern is programmed in a genome, and, like the unconscious cognitive systems of other living beings, it has a centre that enables it to process information, to be spontaneously alive, and to modify phylogenetically acquired knowledge through individual learning processes. He had discovered that the psyche had to be considered a self-regulating system, whose central regulating authority was situated in the unconscious, and that, from this point of view, the ego, which was also spontaneously active, was proved to be a sub-centre.

There were three more theses Jung was able to prove: first, the conscious has developed out of the unconscious. Second, the unconscious contains (a) the programme of the various phases of development of consciousness, and (b) the programme that, each time at the right moment, stimulates its realisation in the process of individuation. Third, the unconscious is capable of being linguistically creative, meaning that (a) it can form symbols that stimulate the ego, but these are symbols which can only be assimilated by the ego after it has worked on them for some time, and (b) the unconscious also contains contents that are not accessible to consciousness: for example, the phylogenetically acquired cognitive and motoric patterns, final values and steps of the programme for the physiological processes, etc.

When working on the theory of depth psychology, I became increasingly aware of the fact that, from my new point of view, the results of biological research converged with the theory of depth psychology. Then I made up my mind to integrate Jung's model of the psyche into the new, enlarged, biological knowledge about living beings, especially about their unconscious cognitive capacity. Indeed, Jung's model could be fitted harmoniously into the biological conception of nature, and it also became obvious that, with hindsight, the results of biological research confirmed Jung's model.

In the context of these various steps of my work, I still had to overcome the second prejudice I had often faced in my discussions in the SHG; this was that there had not been any cultural evolution. I believed that I needed a clear methodical approach to prove that there is an evolution of consciousness. What I especially needed was a measure to describe the degree of the evolutionary level. The methods and approaches of cultural philosophy had proved to be inadequate and useless, and I had to work on an approach that was based on the empirical results of biological research on evolution.

At first, it was necessary to explore the various conceptions of the world of former cultures. After that, I hoped to be able to look at and evaluate the huge amount of information cultural sciences had brought about so far, from my new point of view. To do so, I decided to deepen my knowledge about ethnology and religious studies. Then my first step was to find out if there was a general pattern of understanding ourselves and our world on which all former cultures and religions had been based. I called this general basic pattern "archaic". As this archaic worldview is categorically different from today's view, it can hardly be understood by people now. Therefore, I had to find a way to understand the inner logic of that ancient view. I was convinced that only after having taken these steps would I be able to find a measure to define the degree of the evolutionary level. In order to be able to understand the logic of this archaic view from within, it was instrumental that Jung had discovered that visions did not reveal a supernatural world to us, a world beyond our world here and now, but that the things inwardly perceived in a projection only seem to be so real that they are interpreted concretely. The images perceived are symbolic, metaphorical creations of the unconscious.

The meaningfulness and impact of this discovery for the mutation of consciousness and for today's discussion about the role of religions has hardly been recognised. This discovery makes it obvious that all ideas of concrete supernatural beings, who are believed to be able to influence us and our world acausally and can also reveal themselves to human beings, are the results of a concrete understanding of the creations of the unconscious. But the concrete interpretation of the things perceived in visions was due to those former levels of the evolution of consciousness.

All that means that Jung has principally and scientifically debunked the archaic worldview by discovering that the spontaneous impression deceives the person having a vision. It also means that it will still take a long time until the great majority of people will be able to catch up with this evolutionary step. At the same time, Jung has again opened the religious dimension to people living today, after a long, non-religious phase when the positivistic and materialistic worldview was dominant. Jung was able to open that dimension again because he could explain that the things archaic people had imagined to be supernatural things and persons were actually real, illuminating, effective forces of the psyche, forces superior to the ego. So, it would be appropriate for the ego to display a "religious" attitude towards these forces. This "religiousness", which corresponds to the consciousness of today's evolutionary level, has proved to be "religiousness without religion".

When I described the evolutionary change of the worldview in my first book, I called this evolutionary step "the turning in of the world beyond into the human psyche". Later, I became increasingly aware of the fact that this "turning in" was simply the effect of a more fundamental process: the fundamental change in the conception of objective mental reality.

The exploration of the evolution of consciousness had shown that the separation of mental reality from material reality during the archaic phase was effected by the dualism of this world, here and now, and "the world beyond" because of the fact that the supernatural beings were imagined as being less and less material. It also became obvious that this dematerialisation of supernatural beings approached an infinitesimal limit, just as a mathematical sequence of figures does: this limit was the idea of a being capable of an independent existence, which meant a being that was concrete and, at the same time, purely mental. So, because of the archaic conception of objective mental reality, evolution in the Middle Ages was in danger of hitting the ceiling of any further development. Thus, I had to discover how evolution found a way to a new, no longer concrete, worldview.

At the end of the Middle Ages, the idea of material reality was still quite rudimentary, and the empirical scientific exploration of nature and culture had to catch up with evolution on the physical branch. In the first phase—that is, the Age of Enlightenment—it became evident that reflection on the results of empirical research had led to a purely positivistic, materialistic worldview, which eliminated the idea of supernatural beings who were capable of revealing themselves to people and of intervening arbitrarily in the affairs of this world, here and now. So, the tension grew because the archaic worldview in religions persisted, whereas the point of view of scientists changed rapidly and fundamentally. The extreme tension between these two points of view, which is commonly called the dilemma between knowledge and faith, was only transcended when the unconscious was discovered. It meant that both the archaic and the positivist, materialistic view had to be relativised. Supernature was eliminated, and so a new conception of mental reality had to be looked for in nature. In the meantime, complementary thinking had been developed in the context of microphysical research, and it was no longer necessary to distinguish between matter and mind but, rather, between a material and a mental aspect of a spatio-temporal reality. For the exploration of the mind aspect of nature, or, in other words, for a more differentiated view of nature, materialistically conceived so far, a new methodical approach was helpful. The idea of this approach had come to my mind while working on the dogma of the Assumption. By means of this method, I was now able to explain how, in the course of the entire evolution, objective mental reality as structured energy had developed increasingly complex figurations. Furthermore, I was able to show that, with life coming into existence, another aspect of mental reality fulgurated, and, in addition to life, inwardness appeared, meaning the ability to organise oneself, to process and evaluate data and information. This capability became increasingly complex in the course of biological evolution: for example, when emotional capability and the capacity to experience emerged, and when, finally, the human psyche as the most complex developed form of this structured energy came into being. Other facets of objective mental reality are phenomena that one calls parapsychological, and also the dynamism that manifests itself in individual life as spontaneity and in the evolution of spatio-temporal reality as creativity. This approach allows an explanation of the new paradigm: the mind aspect of nature, which is complementary to the material one. All scientifically proved phenomena, which so far could not be explained by means of the materialistic energy paradigm, could finally be looked at under one theoretical roof.

Besides all these insights, which I could reach through an objectifying attitude when reading Jung, his work was also existentially very rewarding for me. Hence, the way to the process of individuation Jung discovered was very helpful for me, for example. It fostered my efforts to achieve my own psychic maturation, which also includes the awareness of my own mistakes.

Finally, there is one illumination I would like to mention in my concluding words. I received it in my process of individuation, and I think it might enrich psychagogics: my unconscious asked me to give up my attitude of sticking to property and career. In that moment, I suddenly realised that this appeal to me was about the same point that the spiritual master in the Jesuit novitiate had talked about in the days of our spiritual training when he tried to impart Ignatian spirituality. On the one hand, I did not get the point in those days because I was still too busy with the questions of the first part of life, and, on the other hand, I could not understand the deep meaning because the Ignatian insight was presented from the archaic point of view, and I know today that this latter reason seems to have been the more important one.

In any case, I would like to say in these final words that I have become aware of the following phenomena and experiences: while theologians have thought and discussed about the kinds of supernatural beings and their deeds, the schools of spirituality have fostered psychic development and maturation. Through their careful observation of psychic processes of change, they achieved a rich body of knowledge. When I started to explore this know-how and to translate it into the language of the new worldview, it became obvious that all three types of the world religions—the theistic, gnostic, and the cosmological—ultimately have one fundamental aim, in spite of all structural differences. This aim is to become aware of the inner master's voice and listen to, and follow, his instructions and advice. On the way to achieving this aim, a great amount of knowledge about how to proceed was acquired through experience in the course of centuries. After this knowledge was separated from its mythical background, on which its language was based, it proved to be extraordinarily helpful when taking the way of individuation, now against the background of the new worldview. I realised very clearly that it would be highly beneficial to apply this knowledge to psychagogics. The reason is that for hundreds of years our spiritual tradition has decayed because of the constantly growing dominance of the one-sided, irreligious, positivistic, rationalistic attitude, and it seems that we have to start again from zero, as far as spirituality is concerned.

BIBLIOGRAPHY

Alberts, B., & Francisco, F. (1995). *Molecular Biology of the Cell.* New York: Garland.

Albrecht, J. (2007). *Strukturalismus. Ein forschungsgeschichtlicher Überblick.* Tübingen: Narr.

Anderson, J. (2010). *Cognitive Psychology and its Implications.* New York: Worth.

Atkins, P. W. (1994). *The Second Law: Energy, Chaos and Form.* New York: Scientific American Library.

Barrow, J. D. (1988). *The World within the World.* Oxford: Clarendon Press.

Bender, H. (1976). *Verborgene Wirklichkeit. Parapsychologie und Grenzgebiete der Psychologie.* Olten: Walter.

Benz, E. (1969). *Die Vision. Erfahrungsformen und Bilderwelt.* Stuttgart: Klett.

Black Elk (1932). *Black Elk Speaks.* New York: W. Morrow.

Black Elk (1953). *The Sacred Pipe; Black Elk's Account of the Seven Rites of the Oglala Sioux.* Recorded and edited by Joseph Epes Brown. Norman: University of Oklahoma Press.

Blofeld, J. (1973). *The Secret and the Sublime: Taoist Mysteries and Magic.* London: Allen & Unwin.

Brown, P. (1996). *The Rise of Western Christendom: Triumph and Diversity AD 200–1000.* Cambridge, MA: Blackwell.

Bultmann, R. (1993). *Glauben und Verstehen. Gesammelte Aufsätze von R.B. 4 Bde.* Tübingen: Moor.

Burdach, K. (1926). *Reformation, Rennaissace, Humanismus. Zwei Abhandlungen ueber die Grundlage moderner Bildung und Sprachkunst.* Berlin: Paetel.

Carnap, R. (1973). *Grundlagen der Logik und Mathematik.* Munich: Nymphenburger.

Chomsky, N. (1972). *Language and Mind.* New York: Harcourt, Brace, Jovanovich.

Cordan, W. (1977). *Popol Vuh, das Buch des Rates, Mythos und Geschichte der Maya, aus dem Quiché übertragen und erläutert von W. Cordan.* Weimar: Kiepenheuer.

Cramer, F. (1989). *Chaos und Ordnung. Die komplexe Struktur des Lebendigen.* Stuttgart: Deutsche Verlags – Anstalt.

Descartes, R. (2008). *Principles of Philosophy.* New York: Barnes & Noble.

Dulles, A. (1968). *Revelation and Quest for Unity.* Washington, DC: Corpus.

Duve, C. (1995). *Vital Dust: Life as a Cosmic Imperative.* New York: Basic Books.

Eibl-Eibesfeldt, I. (1999). *Grundriss der vergleichenden Verhaltensforschung: Ethologie.* Munich: Piper.

Eigen, M., & Winkler, R. (1975). *Das Spiel. Naturgesetze steuern den Zufall.* Munich: Piper.

Eliade, M. (Ed.) (2002). *Schöpfungsmythen: Ägypter, Sumerer, Hurriter, Hethiter, Kanaaniter und Israeliten.* Düsseldorf: Albatros.

Eliade, M. (2004). *Shamanism: Archaic Techniques of Ecstasy.* Princeton, NJ: Princeton University Press.

Evans-Pritchard, E. E. (1968). *Theories of Primitive Religion.* Oxford: Clarendon Press.

Fasold, H. (1976). *Bioregulation, Regulations- und Kontrollmechanismen in der Zelle.* Heidelberg: Quelle & Meyer.

Freud, S. (1900a). *The Interpretation of Dreams.* S.E., 4–5. London: Hogarth.

Freud, S. (1901b). *The Psychopathology of Everyday Life.* S.E., 6. London: Hogarth.

Freud, S. (1911–1913). *Case History of Schreber, Papers on Technique and Other Works.* S.E., 12. London: Hogarth.

Freud, S. (1913–1914). *Totem and Taboo and Other Works* S.E., 13. London: Hogarth.

Freud, S. (1914–1916). *On the History of the Psycho-Analytic Movement, Papers on Metapsychology and Other Works.* S.E., 14. London: Hogarth.

Freud, S. (1923–1925). *The Ego and the Id and Other Works.* S.E., 19. London: Hogarth.

Freud, S. (1937–1939). *Moses and Monotheism, An Outline of Psycho-Analysis and Other Works. S.E.,* 23. London: Hogarth.

Freundlich, R. (1972). *Einführung in die Semantik.* Darmstadt: WBG.

Gadamer, H. G. (Ed.) (1968). *Um die Begriffswelt der Vorsokratiker.* Darmstadt: WBG.

Glasenapp, H. (1955). *Die Religionen Indiens.* Stuttgart: Kröner.

Granet, M. (1971). *Das chinesische Denken.* Munich: Piper.

Groenbech, V. P. (1932). *The Culture of the Teutons.* London: Oxford University Press.

Gschwend, G. (1998). *Neurophysiologische Grundlagen der Hirnleistungsstörungen.* Basel: S. Karger.

Hawking, S. W., & Mlodinow, L. (2005). *A Briefer History of Time.* New York: Bantam Dell.

Heisenberg, W. (1969). *Der Teil und das Ganze.* Munich: Piper.

Hirschberg, W. (1974). *Die Kulturen Afrikas.* Frankfurt: Athenaion.

Howitt, A. W. (1904). *The Native Tribes of South-East Australia.* London: Macmillan.

Hultkrantz, A. (1953). *Conceptions of the Soul among North American Indians. A Study in Religious Ethnology.* Stockholm: Ethnographical Museum of Sweden.

Jordan, P. (1963). *Die Naturwissenschaftler vor der religiösen Frage.* Oldenburg: Stalling.

Jung, C. G. (1953–1992). *The Collected Works of C. G. Jung,* H. Read, M. Fordham, & G. Adler (Eds.). New York: Pantheon.

Kanitscheider, B. (1996). *Im Innern der Natur. Philosophie der modernen Physik.* Darmstadt: WBG.

Kant, I. (1955). *The Critique of Pure Reason. The Critique of Practical Reason, and Other Ethical Treatises. The Critique of Judgement.* Chicago, IL: Encyclopaedia Britannica.

Kerenyi, K. (1971). *Antike Religion.* Munich: Langen Mueller.

Kuhn, T. S. (1970). *The Structure of Scientific Revolutions.* Chicago, IL: University of Chicago Press.

Kurzrock, R. (1972). *Systemtheorie.* Berlin: Colloquium.

Lévy-Bruhl, L. (1979). *How Natives Think.* New York: Arno.

Lorenz, K. (1973). *Die Rückseite des Spiegels. Versuch einer Naturgeschichte des menschlichen Erkennens.* Munich: Piper.

Müller, W. (1970). *Glauben und Denken der Sioux. Zur Gestalt archaischer Weltbilder.* Berlin: D. Reimer.

Obrist, W. (1980). *Die Mutation des Bewusstseins. Vom archaischen zum heutigen Selbst- und Weltverständnis.* Olten: Peter Lang.

Obrist, W. (1988). *Neues Bewusstsein und Religiositätt. Evolution zum ganzheitlichen Menschen.* Olten: Walter.

Obrist, W. (1990). *Archetypen. Natur- und Kulturwissenschaften bestätigen C.G. Jung.* Olten: Walter.

Obrist, W. (1993). *Tiefenpsychologie und Theologie. Aufbruch in ein neues Bewusstsein.* Zurich: Benziger.

Obrist, W. (1999). *Die Natur – Quelle von Ethik und Sinn. Tiefenpsychologie und heutige Naturerkenntnis.* Zurich: Walter.

Overbeck, F. (1971)[1917]. *Vorgeschichte und Jugend der Scholastik.* Darmstadt: WBG.

Piaget, J. (1971). *Biology and Knowledge; an Essay on the Relations between Organic Regulations and Cognitive Processes.* Chicago, IL: University of Chicago Press.

Plato (1972). *The Works of PLATO, viz. His Fifty-five Dialogues, and Twelve Epistles, translated from the Greek; Nine of the Dialogues by Floyer Sydenham, and the Remainder by Thomas Taylor.* London: printed for T. Taylor by R. Wilks, 1804 [reprinted New York: AMS Press].

Popper, K. R. (1992). *The Logic of Scientific Discovery.* London: Routledge.

Prigogine, I. (1980). *From Being to Becoming: Time and Complexity in the Physical Sciences.* San Francisco, CA: W. H. Freeman.

Schärer, H. (1966). *Der Totenkult der Ngadju Dajak in Sued-Borneo. Bd. I-III.* Leiden: Brill.

Schele, L., & Freidel, D. (1993). *Maya Cosmos: Three Thousand Years on the Shaman's Path.* New York: W. Morrow.

Schopper, H. (1989). *Materie und Antimaterie, Teilchenbeschleuniger und der Vorstoss zum unendlich Kleinen.* Munich: Piper.

Seidel, H. (1994). *Spinoza, zur Einführung.* Hamburg: Junius.

Tuttle, R. H. (Ed.) (1975). *Sociecology and Psychology of Primates.* The Hague: Mouton.

Uexkuell, J. (1921). *Umwelt und Innenwelt der Tiere.* Berlin: Springer.

Ulich, D. (1995). *Das Gefühl. Einführung in die Emotionspsychologie.* Weinheim: Beltz.

Weinberg, S. (1977). *The First Three Minutes: A Modern View of the Origin of the Universe.* New York: Basic Books.

Whorf, B. L. (2012). *Language, Thought, and Reality: Selected Writings of Benjamin Lee Whorf.* Cambridge, MA: MIT Press.

Wiener, N. (1948). *Cybernetics.* New York: Wiley.

INDEX